100 WALKS IN

Cheshire

The Crowood Press

First published in 1990 by
The Crowood Press
Ramsbury
Marlborough
Wiltshire SN8 2HE

British Library Cataloguing in Publication Data
100 walks in Cheshire.
  1. Cheshire. Recreations: Walking
  796.5'1'094271
ISBN 1 85223 357 5

All maps by Philip Smith

Cover pictures by Steven Livingston

Typeset by Carreg Limited, Nailsea, Bristol

Printed in Great Britain by Biddles Ltd, Guildford and King's Lynn

THE CONTRIBUTORS

David Bishop

Mary Dodd

Evelyn Hughes

Tony Kershaw

Steven Livingston

David Meyer

David Miller

Betty Princep

David Thompson

CONTENTS

32. Hale Village and the Mersey Shore 3m (5km)
33. Alvanley and Helsby $3^1/_2$m (6km)
34. Moore Nature Reserve $3^1/_2$m (6km)
35. Dunsdale $3^1/_2$m (6km)
36. Daresbury 4m (6.5km)
37. Willaston and the Wirral Way 4m (6.5km)
38. The Manchester Ship Canal 4m (6.5km)
39. Heswall Village to Parkgate 4m (6.5km)
40. Culcheth and Croft $4^1/_2$m (7.5km)
41. Hatchmere and Kingsley $4^3/_4$m (8km)
42. Burtonwood and the Sankey Valley 5m (8km)
43. The River Weaver 5m (8km)
44. Acton Bridge and Cuddington 5m (8km)
45. Whitegate and the River Weaver $5^1/_4$m (8.5km)
46. Mouldsworth and Manley $5^1/_4$m (8.5km)
47. ...and visiting Mouldsworth Motor Museum $6^1/_4$m (9.75km)
48. Walton and Hill Cliffe $5^1/_2$m (9km)
49. Grappenhall and the Lumb Brook Valley $5^1/_2$m (9km)
50. Barnbridge Gates and Primrose Hill $5^1/_2$m (9km)
51. Great Barrow $5^1/_2$m (9km)

South-West

52. Little Budworth $2^3/_4$m (4km)
53. Farndon and the River Dee 3m (5km)
54. Saighton and Bruera 3m (5km)
55. Chester City Walls 3m (5km)
56. Nantwich and the River Weaver 3m (5km)
57. ...and including Dorfold Hall 4m (6.5km)
58. Marbury and Big Mere $3^1/_4$m (6km)
59. Larkton Hill and Bickerton $3^1/_4$m (6km)
60. Haughton Moss and Bunbury $3^1/_4$m (6km)
61. Chester City Walls and the Meadows 4m (6.5km)
62. Acton to Swanley 4m (6.5km)
63. Beeston Castle and the Peckforton Woods $4^1/_2$m (7.5km)
64. Malpas and Overton Heath $4^3/_4$m (8km)
65. Guilden Sutton and Christleton 5m (8km)
66. Nantwich, Hurleston and Acton 5m (8km)
67. Aston juxta Mondrum and Barbridge $5^1/_2$m (9km)

68. Gallantry Bank and Bulkeley Hill $5^1/_2$m (9km)
69. Whitchurch and Wirswall 6m (9.5km)
70. Around Wrenbury $6^1/_2$m (10km)
71. Higher and Lower Wych $6^1/_2$m (10km)
72. Taporley and Wharton's Lock $6^1/_2$m (10km)
73. Aldford and the River Dee $6^3/_4$m (11km)
74. Primrose Hill and Willington corner $6^3/_4$m (11km)
75. Chester Canal and Welsh Canal $8^1/_2$m (13.5km)

South-East

76. Danebridge 2m (3km)
77. Hough and Wybunbury 3m (5km)
78. Rode Mill and Little Moreton Hall $3^1/_2$m (6km)
79. Around Church Minshull $3^1/_2$m (6km)
80. …and alternative route $4^1/_2$m (7km)
81. Astbury $3^1/_2$m (6km)
82. Alsager and the Merelake Way $3^3/_4$m (6km)
83. The Vale of Audlem 4m (6.5km)
84. North Rode 4m (6.5km)
85. Barthomley and Englesea Brook $4^1/_2$m (7.5km)
86. Wybunbury and Hatherton 5m (8km)
87. Brereton Green 5m (8km)
88. Timbersbrook and The Cloud $5^1/_4$m (8.5km)
89. Timbersbrook and Ravensclough $5^1/_4$m (8.5km)
90. Wheelock and Moston $5^1/_2$m (8.5km)
91. Winterley $5^1/_2$m (9km)
92. Ackers Crossing and Mow Cop $5^1/_2$m (9km)
93. Astbury $6^1/_2$m (10km)
94. Swettenham $6^1/_2$m (10km)
95. Hankelow and Broomhall $7^1/_2$m (12km)
96. Hanging Gate and the Gritstone Trail 8m (13km)
97. Holmes Chapel and Bradwall $8^1/_2$m (13.5km)
98. Warmingham Moss $8^3/_4$m (14km)
99. Church Minshull and Wettenhall 9m (14.5km)
100. Around Bridgemere 12m (19km)

INTRODUCTION

The Crowood Press are greatly indebted to our contributors who walked cheerfully all over the county researching the walks for this book. It must be borne in mind that while all the details of these walks (hedges, fences, stile, and so on) were correct at the time of going to print, the countryside is constantly changing and we cannot be held responsible if details in the walk descriptions are found to be inaccurate. We would be grateful if walkers would let us know of any major alterations to the walks described so that we may incorporate any changes in future editions. Please write to THE 100 WALKS SERIES, The Crowood Press, Crowood House, Ramsbury, Marlborough, Wiltshire SN8 2HE. Walkers are strongly advised to take with them the relevant map for the area and Ordnance Survey maps are recommended for each walk. The walks are organised by dividing the county arbitrarily into four areas – north-east, north-west, south-west and south-east – and are then listed by length – from approximately 2 miles to 12 miles. No attempt has been made to estimate how long the walks will take as this can vary so greatly depending on the strength and fitness of the walkers and the time spent exploring the points of interest highlighted. Nearly all the walks are circular and the majority offer a recommended place to seek refreshments. Telephone numbers of these pubs and cafés are included in case you want to check on opening times, meals available, and so on.

We hope you enjoy exploring the county of Cheshire in the best possible way – on foot – and ask that you cherish its beautiful places by always remembering the country code:

Enjoy the country and respect its life and work
Guard against all risk of fire
Fasten all gates
Keep dogs under close control
Keep to public footpaths across all farmland
Use gates and stiles to cross field boundaries
Take your litter home
Help to keep all water clean
Protect wildlife, plants and tress
Make no unnecessary noise

Good walking.

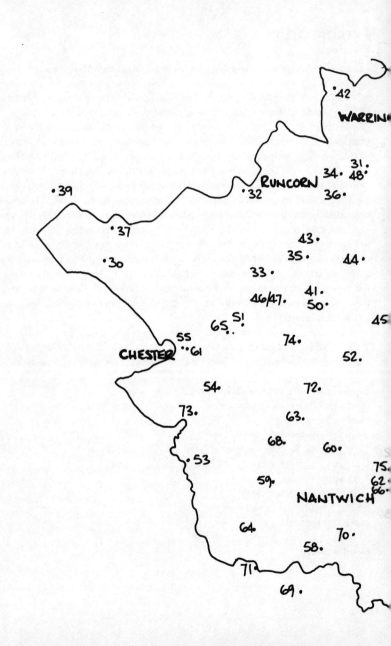

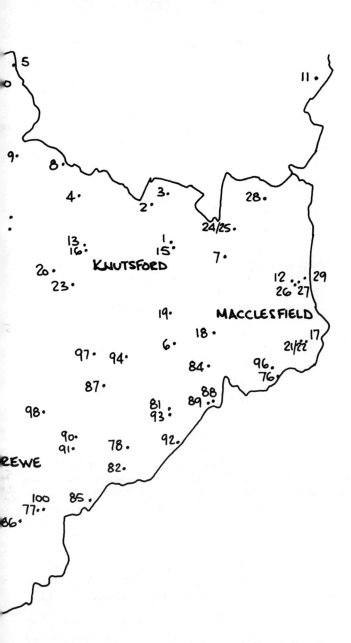

Walk 1   **ALDERLEY EDGE AND HOUGH**   3m (5km)

Maps: OS Sheets Landranger 118; Pathfinder SJ 87/97.

A walk involving some climbing, but otherwise not strenuous. On the edge beware as route finding can be difficult.

Start: At 859773, the National Trust car park on the B5087.

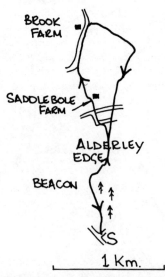

From the car park head towards the Information Centre. Turn right just in front of this building and go forwards down the National Trust private road for a very short distance before turning left in front of The Bungalow and along a well-maintained track. When you enter a clearing ahead, go straight across it to join a path which bears to the left. Continue ahead over cross-tracks and at the next cross-tracks, just before a stone wall, bear right and uphill towards the remains of the Armada Beacon. From the Beacon turn your back on the stone wall and go down a track ahead, following this until you can branch off right to an open, rocky viewpoint. The views from here extend from the Welsh hills to the west to the Derbyshire Peak District to the east on a clear day. You will also find some **caves** here but take care if you do go into them, particularly if you have children with you. When you return to the main path go straight ahead passing one yellow bridleway marker, then ahead on a path to the left of the next yellow bridleway marker which lies 10 yards further on. Following this path when at the bottom of a dip, at an intersection of paths, bear sharp left on to a downhill track then right 10 yards further on. This path emerges at a barbed wire fence and a field, turn left here and follow the path to the road. Turn left then right at the road to follow the Public Footpath sign to Saddlebole Farm. At the end of the drive go left over a stile to enter a field. Keep the hedge on your right and when it ends in 20 yards turn right and follow a track to the road ahead. At the road turn right and after 550 yards turn right again down a footpath signposted 'Mottram' which lies opposite the entrance to Brook Farm. Walk across a field, bearing left to join a hedge, and just past a pool behind this hedge is a waymarked stile which you cross and then you turn right. Cross a stile ahead and turn right again following a sign for **'The Edge'**. Cross a footbridge and a stile and go left in the field, keeping the hedge on your immediate left to go over two more stiles and so on to the road. Over the road is an upward path and where this enters a wood take any of the paths going up as they should all lead back near to the open rocky outcrop. Now retrace your steps to the Armada Beacon and the car park.

POINTS OF INTEREST:
The caves – They date back to the early 18th century when mainly copper ore was mined here.
Alderley Edge – 600ft high with excellent views of the Cheshire Plain. There was once a Neolithic settlement here. Bronze Age pottery and tools have been discovered in this area.

REFRESHMENTS:
The Wizard, Alderley Edge (tel no: 0625 584000). Tea room at the back open on Saturday and Sunday 12 - 6pm for sandwiches and snacks. Children welcome. Dogs allowed in outside area only.
There are a variety of pubs, cafés and restaurants in Alderley Edge.

Walk 2   **THE BOLLIN AND MORLEY** $3^1/_2$m (6km)

Maps: OS Sheets Landranger 109; Pathfinder SJ 88/98.

An easy walk on well-maintained tracks. It can be combined with a visit to Styal which is well worthwhile.

Start: At 840822, the car park on the B5166 in Wilmslow.

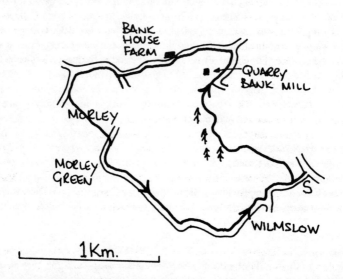

From the car park follow the distinct path leading north, with the River Bollin on your left and the toilets on your right, to cross Twinnies Bridge and enter the National Trust area. Now simply keep to the path with the river still on your left all the way to **Quarry Bank Mill**. (See the National Trust map at Twinnies Bridge for details as these paths are concessionary and many do not appear on the OS map.) Keep on the main tarmac track through the mill buildings and then look for a signpost saying 'Footpath to Morley' on the left. The sign indicates you follow an old cobbled packhorse road leading down, over the river and straight ahead to Bank House Farm. The main part of **Styal Country Park** is to the right here.

    Go forwards through the farm yard and down the farm road to the main road where you turn right and then left at the first junction, signposted 'Morley Green and

Mobberley'. After 100 yards turn left at a sign marked 'Nan's Moss Lane and Wilmslow'. Enter a field by a stile and bear left to another stile 15 yards to the left of a large tree, then ahead to a further stile and a minor road. Turn right here and follow the road for 200 yards then go left opposite Moss Grove Farm down a grassy track signposted 'Wilmslow'. At a crossing of tracks carry straight on eventually to join a road, then turn left and keep ahead to the main road (A538). Cross this road and keep ahead down a path opposite, signposted to 'King's Road and Twinnies Bridge'. Ignore the next signpost for Twinnies Bridge and keep straight ahead over a bridge. Turn left at the road and then right down Broadwalk and left again 20 yards ahead down a track to Pownall Hall Farm. Do not miss the green Victorian letter box which you pass on the way. Continue straight along this track and then left at the road and right down a bridle path just before you reach the Rugby Club. Follow this bridle path back to the car park.

POINTS OF INTEREST:
Quarry Bank Mill – Founded in 1784 as a water-powered cotton spinning mill. Now run as a working museum and also open to the public, June - September daily 11 - 5pm. The rest of the year not open on Mondays, other days 11 - 4pm or 5pm. Open Bank Holidays (tel no: 0625 527468).
Styal Country Park – Woodland walks through the park, including the Apprentices Walk via Twinnies Bridge and Wilmslow. The estate, built for mill owners and workers, belongs to the National Trust. Open to the public.

REFRESHMENTS:
The Mill Kitchen, Quarry Bank Mill (tel no: 0625 527468). Serves home-cooked food, lunches and teas. Open only when the mill is. There is also a Pie Shop open in summer. There are cafés, pubs and restaurants in Wilmslow for refreshments.

Walk 3   STYAL AND QUARRY BANK MILL   3¹/₂m (6km)

Maps: OS Sheets Landranger 109; Pathfinder SJ 88/98.

An easy walk, with a couple of short steep climbs, through farmland and a beautiful wooded valley. Muddy after rain.

Start: At 836836, the National Trust car park in Styal village.

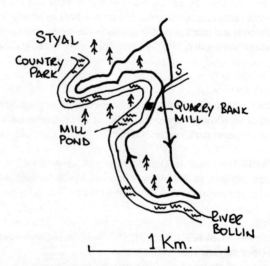

Leave the car park by the footpath in the bottom right-hand corner. Then turn left alongside some cottages which are part of **Styal model village**. Just beyond the National Trust office, take a cobbled path left, passing the old village cross, on to the footpath signposted Quarry Bank Mill. Keep straight ahead at a rough track and when you reach a metalled road cross and turn right along a footpath which skirts the Quarry Bank Mill car park. This is signposted the Apprentices Way. Cross two stiles to leave the car park and follow a well-trodden path through several fields. Where the footpath begins to descend over cobbles. Turn right down a grassy slope to a kissing gate. This returns to National Trust property and leads through splendidly attractive woodland. At a junction of paths, bear right uphill. A short climb leads to a footbridge over a gully and down on your left is the River Bollin. (The riverbank path here is at present unusable due to work on the mill pond down river. Until this changes, take the following alternative.) Bear right away from the river; this footpath runs parallel to it, higher up. After passing the mill pond and the weir, it climbs once more, towards a large building ahead. This is Quarry Bank Mill (see Walk 2) and refreshments are available here in the Mill Kitchen. To continue the walk, climb steadily uphill along the road from the mill. Just short of the car park, take a footpath on your left, signposted 'To the Woods'. After crossing a rough track, turn left at a path junction (signposted 'Woods'). This drops steeply above a deep gully and soon you will reach some steps which descend to the River Bollin. Turn right here along the river bank. The footpath now follows the river around a big loop. One hundred yards after passing a footbridge across the Bollin, leave the river and take a path steeply uphill. This eventually levels out and contours above another deep gully. When you reach a barrier, turn right down some steps, descending into the gully and eventually crossing it by a stone bridge. Climb some steps on the other side, bearing left by another barrier, then climb steadily, emerging out of the woods through a pinch gap. Go straight across a rough track here. The footpath beyond leads past a chapel on to a cobbled road. Keep straight ahead here into the main street of Styal village. If you require refreshment, turn right to reach the Ship Inn. To return to the car park, turn left.

POINTS OF INTEREST:

Styal model village – Built in the 1820s by enlightened mill owner, Samuel Greg, to house his expanding workforce. Greg was concerned that his employees should live close to the mill and in an attractive environment, so he built several terraces of picturesque cottages, together with a church, shop and school. Although the village shop is no longer in business, there is an interesting display of the products which would have been sold there at the turn of the century.

REFRESHMENTS:
The Ship Inn, Styal (tel no: 0625 523818).
The Mill Kitchen, Quarry Bank Mill (tel no: 0625 527468).

Walk 4   **ROSTHERNE** $3\frac{1}{2}$m (6km)

Maps: OS Sheets Landranger 109; Pathfinder SJ 68/78.

A most interesting walk through farmlands, church grounds, and alongside Rostherne Mere.

Start: At 726837, in the lane going north-west from Bucklow Hill village.

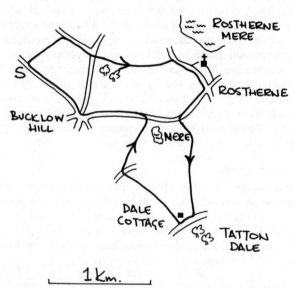

Take the footpath that begins through a gateway on the right at the side of a tall hedgerow. The way is forward along a field track with a hedge on the right emerging on to a crossing lane by the side of a cottage. Turn right and shortly cross the main road, then go forward down the entrance drive of Denfield Hall Farm. Pass through two gates and turn left before the farmhouse to enter a field through a kissing gate. Bear right and go forward with a hedge on the right to keep in line with the church tower ahead, passing through a second gap in a facing hedge descending steps to join a lane. Cross a bridge over a stream, and climb the hill to **Rostherne Church** reached through a revolving lych gate. Leave the church porch, and, bearing left, cross the church grounds along a path through a gate on to a track. Go through two more gates and meet a crossing lane, then walk straight ahead down the opposite lane for $1/4$ mile. Turn left through a kissing gate just before the lane descends, and go forward along a field track, turning right at a facing hedge through a second kissing gate. Take the footpath diagonally left across the facing field, pass through another kissing gate, and head towards farm buildings across the field. As the buildings are almost reached, Tatton Hall can be seen down an avenue of trees straight ahead. Through a further kissing gate turn right along the road, pass farm buildings on the left of Dale Cottage (1626) on the right, go right through a field gate after the cottage and walk forward with a hedge on the right. The hedge turns right shortly but keep straight ahead to pass over a crossing fence then forward with a fence on the right, crossing a stile at the side of a facing field gate. Now go right and immediately cross a second stile. Turn left and then go forward to pass through a field gate by a small dwelling, turning right on to a lane. Pass in front of a cottage, then turn left to descend and pass over a stream and stile. Climb again, bearing right and cross a stile at the end of a field gate. Go forward with a hedge on the left and cross a stile in a facing fence. Turn right descending close to the mere, go over a stile to meet a lane, turn left and follow the lane for almost half a mile. Go right at the junction ahead, arriving by the Swan Hotel. Walk over the main road, and down Chapel Lane to your car.

POINTS OF INTEREST:
Rostherne Church – The church has a sandstone tower built in 1742 which replaced the earlier steeple built in 1533.

REFRESHMENTS:
None really available, unless you can change your hiking boots and call in at the Swan Hotel.

Walk 5   GLAZEBURY AND HITCHFIELD WOOD   4m (6.5km)

Maps: OS Sheets Landranger 109; Pathfinder SJ 69/79.

An easy walk, fairly level across fields and through woodland. Muddy in some sections after rain.

Start: At 673971, the car park opposite the church in Glazebury.

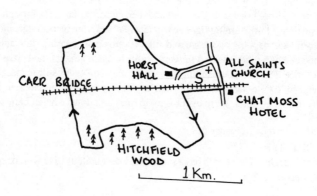

From the car park turn left on to the A574 and go under the railway bridge. On your left is the **Chat Moss Hotel**. Opposite this take a footpath along the edge of the **Manchester and Liverpool Railway**. After passing through a gap turn left along the hedge. Where this ends keep straight ahead for 200 yards, and turn right along a footpath which crosses the field to a footbridge. On the other side turn right over a stile and follow the stream. A further stile takes you into Hitchfield Wood. For the next $1/_2$ mile the path meanders through the wood. It is not a public right of way but a permissive footpath, and access to the final section of the wood is barred, so leave by a stile and turn right along the wood edge, bearing to the left to reach a signpost. Turn right here over a stile and keep straight ahead to reach a rough track. Turn right along this, under the railway and then straight across a field to a kissing gate. Here follow the fence on the left and,

22

just before reaching a stile, turn right across the field, towards a clump of trees. Pass around these on the left, and continuing in the same direction make for some more, surrounding a large pond. After passing this on the left, you will reach a footbridge. Cross this and bear diagonally left across a field, following a fence around a marshy area to your right. When you reach a stile, turn right to another footbridge. Cross this and keep straight ahead towards Hurst Hall. Soon the footpath becomes a rough tarmacked road which leads past the farm on to the farm access road. Turn left along this to its junction with the A574 in Glazebury. To return to the car park, turn right past All Saints Church.

POINTS OF INTEREST:

Chat Moss Hotel – This was the original booking office of Glazebury Station, and the ticket window can still be seen. The name recalls Chat Moss, over which the railway crossed, the track built on bales of cotton sunk into the spongy ground.

The Manchester and Liverpool Railway – This was the first passenger railway in the world, built by George Stephenson in 1830.

REFRESHMENTS:

The Chat Moss Hotel, Glazebury (tel no: 092 576 2128).

Walk 6   **MARTON**   4m (6.5km)

Maps: OS Sheets Landranger 118; Pathfinder SJ 86/96.

A walk through some of Cheshire's finest dairy farming pastures.

Start: At 852674, in the lane to Rodeheath just south of Marton off the A34. Park on the left-hand side by a footpath sign.

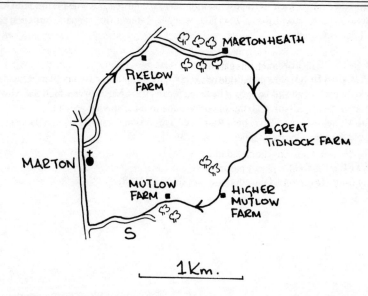

Leaving the car, walk back to the A34, and turn right in the direction of **Marton Church**. Cross the road opposite the church and go over a stile where a sign indicates the way to Swettenham. Cross a facing field, then with a hedge on your right climb over two stiles to enter a lane. Go right, following the lane as it winds past a farm and black and white cottage, arriving at a crossing road. Follow the sign indicating 'Gasworth 3 miles', continue past a lane on your right and keep straight on for $^1/_2$ mile to arrive at Pikelow Farm on the right. Shortly after passing the farm turn right to enter Martonheath Farm approach track; on the right are the ponds of the trout farm. Follow the track as it takes you through woods and when you arrive at a cottage on your left the way is forward along a grassy track arriving at a facing field gate. Go through the gate and along a field edge with a fence on your right, and pass through a second gate, to go along a well-defined track. Continue through three more gates, and at the third gate, which is close to Tidnock farmhouse, bear diagonally right to cross the farmyard. Continue for a short distance along a track, and go right through a field gate with a fence on your immediate right. Carry on along level ground at first, and follow a half-hidden track that descends then bears left. Go forward through a small facing gate then cross a stream via a footbridge. Continue with a line of trees on your right.

After the trees end go right through a field gap, and continue until Higher Mutlow Farm can be seen on the left. Keeping a hedge to your right, pass through a facing gate close to the farmhouse, continue through the farmyard and go through another facing gate leading on to a track that bears right then left through a gateway to meet a further gate. Do not go through this gate but turn right through another gate to arrive at Mutlow Farm. Fork left here to the side of farm buildings and continue, passing a pond on the left. The track leads on to a crossing lane where the way is right. Follow the lane for $^1/_2$ mile to arrive back at your car.

POINTS OF INTEREST:
Marton Church – Founded in 1343. Reputed to be one of the finest timber churches in England with a most unusual wooden tile covering on the tower and bell chamber. Inside the church are two interesting effigies said to be of Sir John Davenport and his son.

Walk 7   **PRESTBURY**   4m (6.5km)

Maps: OS Sheets Landranger 118; Pathfinder SJ 87/97.

A walk over farmlands, down lanes, and through a lovely old Cheshire village. The fields can be very muddy in wet weather.
Start: At 902771, near Pearl Street, Prestbury.

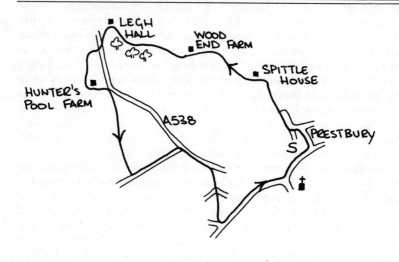

1 Km.

Go left out of the car park by the Way Out sign, then right along Bollin Grove, and enter a track skirting a sports field. The track now bears left and goes over a bridge, crossing the river Bollin. Follow the track as it winds right, and continue until, just before the entrance of Spittle House, there is a stile by a field gate on your left. Cross the stile and, keeping a fence to your right, follow a facing path which bears right. Cross a fence close to a large tree, and then, with a row of trees on the right, descend and turn right through a gap in the trees. Bear left and go over a stile, cross a stream, and then climb keeping a fence on the left. Go over a stile on your left at the side of a gate, walk forward to the left of facing farm outbuildings and go right past the buildings. Continue with a fence on your left. On meeting a facing holly hedge turn left over a stile, climb and enter a grassy track, then pass a farm approach track to a stile in the opposite hedge. On crossing this stile keep forward and descend across rough open ground. Climb up a facing bank keeping to the right of trees, and with a hedge on the left descend and cross a stile at the side of an old wooden gate. Walk forward along a field edge, go over a crossing fence and turn right on meeting a facing hedge. Follow the hedge until you come to a metal field gate, pass through the kissing gate at the left of the field gate and then go right, following a cobbled track between outbuildings. Keep to the track, which bears left to pass Legh Hall and a pool on the right to arrive at a crossing road.

Turn left, then immediately right to enter a track leading to Hunters Pool Farm. Pass through the farm entrance gate, and cross the farmyard to go through a second gate on to a tarmac drive. At a crossing road on your right in a couple of yards you will see a footpath sign. Walk to a stile straight ahead at the left-hand side of a facing gate, where there is a small pond on the left. Keep forward past a corner hedge on the left-hand side and continue across a facing field. Keep in the same direction as before and aim for houses which are about $1/4$ mile away straight ahead. Go over a double stile in a crossing fence, and with a hedge on the left cross a stile leading on to a lane. Turn left, and follow the lane past large houses to arrive at a T-junction. Turn right, walking for $1/4$ mile to arrive at Castlegate, where you turn right to descend to a junction. Enter a facing footpath between hedges, bear left over a stile and turn to cross a stream. Climb to a crossing lane where the way is left, then turn left at a T-junction. This is Chelford Lane. Continue with a golf course on the right and large houses on the left. At a T-junction turn right and then left into Prestbury village, noting the fine black and white timbered building which has been restored and is now in use as a bank. Go past Bradford Lane, where it becomes cobbled and leads to a fork. Turn left here to climb past Bradford House Farm and Bradford Lodge Nurseries, then next left to the T-junction ahead. Turn left here and cross the road back to your car.

REFRESHMENTS:
Several available in the village.

Walk 8   BOLLINGTON AND BERRISTALL DALE   4 $\frac{1}{2}$m (7.5km)

Maps: OS Sheets Landranger 118; Pathfinder SJ 87/97.

A walk through hilly terrain with some splendid views. Wellingtons or boots advised.

Start: At 937779, the car park in Bollington, just off the B5090.

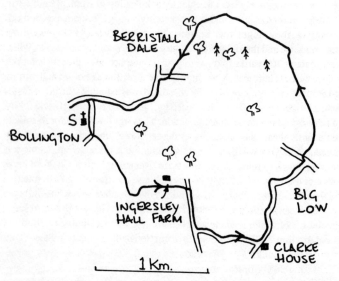

Leave the car park by the main entrance and turn left at the main road. Continue uphill and right into Church Street passing the **St John's Church** on your right. At a T-junction turn left, passing small factories on your left. Fifty yards after the last factory cross a stile on the left with a Gritstone Trail marker. Cross the bridge in the field and then follow an obvious track uphill and to the left (once a path used by mill workers walking into Bollington). Squeeze through a stile and go forward with a wall on your left. Big Low will come into view directly ahead, and you continue straight on over fields and stiles, ignoring a Gritstone Trail marker when it indicates sharp left, until you reach a wide gateway. Cross the adjacent stile and turn right on to a farm track which you follow uphill for approximately $\frac{1}{4}$ mile. Fifty yards before the top of the rise turn left through a gate (not waymarked) and go straight ahead on a well-defined track with the wall on your left. (If this track is too wet and difficult for you, follow the track you have just left and turn left down a road to Clarke House.) Go through the farmyard to join a minor road, turn left, and then right at a T-junction to join a fairly busy road. Turn left and then immediately right at a way mark sign. Take the right-hand of two tracks – downhill – and follow this for 500 yards. Just past a stone building on the left cross a stile, also on the left, and go to the right, continuing downhill to cross a low stone wall and a fence just to the right of a large holly bush. Keep the hedge and fence on your right, then, where they bend away to the right, keep straight on and cross a stile. Cut through the farmyard to a gate on the right, and follow the track on the other side which leads downhill and over two footbridges, then bears right uphill to a stile and a wooden gate. Carry on up the short rise and then continue straight ahead and gently uphill on a wide, surfaced track for about 700 yards, until you go over a second cattle grid. Bear left to a telegraph pole in the field before the farm, and then carry on downhill to cross a bridge. Turn left and cross the wall ahead and continue down on a distinct path. Cross a stile bearing a Gritstone Trail way mark and then a packhorse bridge. Bear sharp left, uphill, to the top and follow the track over stiles and fields to a minor road. Turn right here to join a road some yards ahead, passing the Cheshire Hunt on your right where you can stop for refreshment if you wish. Turn left at the road and follow the signs for **Bollington** into the town, to rejoin the B5090 and the car park.

POINTS OF INTEREST:

St John's Church – Consecrated in 1834 by the Bishop of Chester. The churchyard has 10 war graves, all of which are maintained by the War Graves Commission.
Bollington – A former mill town with many stone houses. There was also extensive quarrying around Bollington of Kerridge free stone, valued for its whiteness. From it the nave of Christ Church, Oxford, and also the promenade gardens of Douglas on the Isle of Man are made.

REFRESHMENTS:

The Cheshire Hunt Inn, Hedgerow, Rainow (tel no: 0625 73185). En route and serving hot meals and snacks daily from 12-3pm. Mention children if booking. No dogs.
The Cock and Pheasant, Bollington (tel no: 0625 73289). Bar snacks and hot dishes Monday-Saturday. Food served from 12-2pm. Children welcome, but no dogs.
The Country Café, Rainow (tel no: 0625 73357). Closed Monday and Friday, otherwise open at 12.45 for set lunch and lighter meals. Book in advance. Teas available 3.30-6pm, except Monday. Children welcome, but no dogs.

Walk 9   LYMM   4 ¹/₂ m (7.5km)

Maps: OS Sheets Landranger 109; Pathfinder SJ 68/78.

A leisurely walk alongside the Bridgewater Canal and Lymm Dam.

Start: At 683873, the car park, Pepper Street, Lymm.

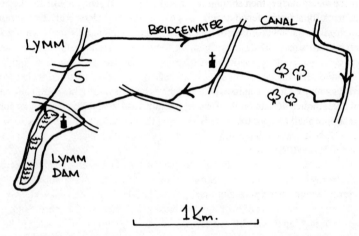

Leaving the car park, turn right and pass Lymm Cross, an old sandstone monument, then turn right again to follow the road for a short distance to a hump-back bridge over the **Bridgewater Canal**. Go over this bridge and turn right to follow the canal towpath. After almost a mile, pass under two bridges. Shortly after the second bridge the canal passes over a lane. Descend some steps here to leave the canal side and walk under the bridge. Follow the lane, bearing right and after 300 yards on the right side of the road, turn through a field gate, then continue with a hedge on the left. The path shortly turns right, and then left, past a deep-set pond to enter a wood. Carry on through trees to emerge into a field, where you continue with a hedge on the left in the direction of the church spire ahead. Go through a kissing gate to enter a lane, turn left and pass the church to turn right down a narrow fenced-in path that starts at the side of a field gate.

Follow the path across the fields and turn right at the lane ahead. Go forward at the junction ahead and pass between railings to proceed with the fence on the right and houses on the left. The path shortly joins a road where the way is right in the direction of St Mary's Church, which can be seen straight ahead. Enter a fenced-in path between houses to emerge on to a road opposite the church. Cross the road and follow the path which starts at the right-hand side of the church grounds and leads to the water's edge of Lymm Dam. Carry on for 200 yards then climb to the left and proceed along higher ground to converge towards a tree-lined track. Continue along this track which shortly bears right over a bridge. Turn right immediately after crossing the bridge and follow the path between two concrete posts. The path continues with trees on the right, passes close to the water's edge, then shortly meets a road where the way is straight ahead through a gap in a facing fence and down some steps then along a pathway with overhanging trees. You will emerge on to a road in the centre of **Lymm** village. Turn right and follow the road, which bears left then climbs back to Lymm Cross and the car.

POINTS OF INTEREST:
The Bridgewater Canal – Engineered by James Brindley to distribute coal from the Duke of Bridgewater's estates at Worsley near Manchester. Completed in 1767, it runs through Grappenhall to enter the Mersey through a series of locks at Runcorn.
Lymm – There are many interesting old buildings, and the village was built on a massive bed of sandstone rock.

REFRESHMENTS:
Available in Lymm village pubs and cafés.

Walk 10   **ARLEY**   4 $\frac{1}{2}$m (7.5km)

Maps OS Sheets Landranger 109; Pathfinder SJ 68/78.

A level walk over farmlands and lanes, very muddy in rain.

Start: At 692806, on the road between High Legh and Great
Budworth near Litley Farm Park.

Proceed down a bridleway marked 'Private road public footpath only', noting the
Sign, and pass through a gate at the side of a lodge house, and on down a wooded lane.
Turn right just before the gate of a second lodge house, and cross Arley Brook to enter
the hamlet of Arley Green. Carry on past an old water pump on the right, and follow
the cobbled path, part of the original road to the Hall. Pass a lane on the right, and
continue with trees on the left to turn next right down a rough track, signposted to High
Legh. Pass a 'Private' road on the left, then leave the track to the right of a small bridge
which carries the track to the left over a field. From here follow the right side of a facing
ditch for 200 yards, then go left over a stile and footbridge to enter a field. Turn right
and keep forward to pass over a stile at the right-hand side of a crossing hedge. After
a short distance the fence on the right turns away to the right but the footpath is

diagonally left, passing two trees to join a stile at the approach to a footbridge over the M6. Cross the motorway then turn right along Hobbs Hill Lane to pass two lanes on the left, walking on to Arley View Farm on the right. Carry on past dwellings on the left, and turn right at the T-junction ahead. This lane turns left shortly but carry straight on, passing to the right of Northwood Cottage and on past a 'Private' road to Northwood House to arrive at a facing gate. Pass through this gate, and, with a hedge on the right, pass through a further two gates to reach another footbridge over the motorway. Cross the motorway and go through a gate following a track straight ahead between trees to a facing gate. Do not go through this gate but take the path to the right which leads through woodland. Shortly the path turns left and enters a lane at the left of a group of 16th-century cottages. Turn right, go down a winding lane, passing once again over Arley Brook, and turn left at the next junction to go back to the car.

PLACES OF INTEREST:
Sign – Note the sign at the beginning of the walk by the bridleway:
> *'This road forbidden is to All*
> *Unless they wend their way to call*
> *At mill or Arley Green'*

You can imagine Arley Green Spring Festival of May Day being celebrated around a maypole set in the centre of the Arley Green.

Take time to stop and browse, as parts of this walk seem to have changed little over the centuries.

REFRESHMENTS:
No refreshments available, so take a flask.

Walk 11   MOTTRAM AND BROADBOTTOM   5m (8km)

Maps: OS Sheets Landranger 109 and 110; Pathfinder SJ 89/99 and SK 09/19.

Farmland, Pennine views, industrial archaeology and woodland.

Start: At 993955, the village green, Mottram in Longdendale.

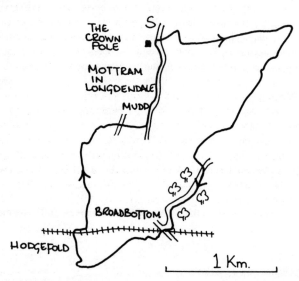

Go through the car park to the right of the White Hart. Go over a stile and keep right through a farmyard. Follow the farm track to a stile in the right corner of a field. Go over and shortly find steps on the left. Descend, cross the cemetery to a stile and cross it. Bear slightly left to another stile on the far side of a field. Cross the next field to follow the fence at its right edge to a stile. Cross and pass to the right of bushes. Cross a stream, then climb and go over a stile. Cross a field to trees at the far left and follow them to a stile by the farmhouse. A path leads along the garden fence, then through a hedge on to a lane. Cross, go over a stile, and cross a field to a bridge, just over the brow. Cross the next field to a stile under the middle of a group of three bushes at the far edge. Turn right, to follow the edge of the next field to a gap in the corner. Turn right to a bridge. Cross and follow the fence on the right to a stile. Cross and keep to the hedge until a farm track is crossed. Go over a stile, cross a field to another, then head uphill to a post. A little further on, a stile leads to the end of Pingot Lane.

Keep right along the lane, and after passing under power lines cross a stile, left, and follow a hedge down to Hague Lane. Go right and follow it to Broadbottom. Go left under the railway and cross the road under the arch to pass right of the Community Centre. Go down steps to Mill Brow. Go to the bottom of Mill Brow and turn right on to Well Row. This becomes a rocky path, climbing steeply on to Hodge Lane. Follow this past **Summerbottom Cottages**, and beyond the renovated Dye Vats turn left on to a road. At the far end of Hodge Fold Cottages turn right. Follow a stream to steps on the left. At the top, turn right, go through a gate and follow a path through woods to a railway bridge. Go over and turn right to follow the railway until the path forks left to follow the brook far below to your left. This is Hurst Clough. The path descends to the brook, crosses it, then re-crosses it. Go up and take the second major path on your right leading on up. Shortly, turn left sharply back on yourself. This leads, via a right fork, back to the brook again. Some distance later, cross the brook and take a right fork upwards. Some steps take you up and out of the Clough. Once out of the woods, follow the path gently upwards, keeping right, up to Broadbottom Road. Cross the road, and pass through a gate at the back of the 'Waggon' car park. Follow the path, beneath the power cables, via three stiles on to Littlemoor Road. Turn left and follow the road to the church. Bear right between farmhouses, to arrive at the gate to **Mottram Church**. Turn left down a cobbled path, then follow the church boundary wall to the right. After a grassy path and some more cobbles, a flight of steps lead back down Church Brow to the **Crown Pole**.

POINTS OF INTEREST:

Summerbottom Cottages – Broadbottom was an industrial village, the River Etherow turning waterwheels. Summerbottom Cottages are handloom weavers cottages, survivors of a period when entire families would work on the raw materials distributed to homes. **Mottram Church** – Rebuilt in the 15th century. In the churchyard, beware Captain Whittle's wind, which blew that gentleman's coffin out of its bearers' grasp. Stop and read the inscription on the Bodysnatcher's Tombstone, that of 15-year-old Lewis Brierley, buried in 1827, '*Though once beneath the ground his corpse was laid, For use of Surgeons it was thence conveyed...*'
The Crown Pole – Erected in 1925 to replace an earlier wooden one.

REFRESHMENTS:
The Packhorse Inn (tel no: 0457 63928).

Walk 12   LAMALOAD   5m (8km)

Maps OS Sheets Landranger 118; Pathfinder SJ 87/97.

A moderately strenuous walk over well-defined terrain.

Start: At 976753, the car park on the east side of Lamaload reservoir.

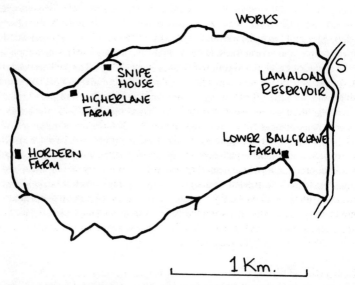

Leave the car park at the back, head towards the reservoir past the public lavatories on your left and then turn right and down a track to cross a stile by a gate. A grass track to the right of the reservoir leads eventually to a large hole in the wall from where you can see your next objective, the Water Board houses, at the bottom of the hill. Turn left at the bottom, passing the gates marked 'Private' on your right. Go over the bridge crossing the stream and then immediately cross a stile. Turn right and follow the direction of the Public Footpath sign along a muddy track between stone walls. Just before a gate, fork right down a paved way and turn left at the Water Board's road which you follow for about 1 mile, passing first Snipe House Farm and then Higherlane Farm on the left. At this point the road drops down and as you pass a group of houses on the left, **White Nancy** comes into view on the right. A sharp right turn leads to a gradual ascent. 50 yards beyond the next row of houses on the left cross a stone stile in the wall, also on the left. Walk diagonally left and through a gap in a wall by the back gate of the last house you recently passed. Turn right and continue uphill. The climb is broken by a dilapidated stile in a wall ahead, and once over the stile you continue upwards with the wall on your immediate right. Cross a stile on the right before you reach a tumbledown wall and go left, diagonally, to cross a ladder stile next to an iron gate. On the other side turn right, continue along a farm track to Hordern Farm and go straight through the farmyard. A stone stile, next to a gate beyond the farm buildings, gives on to a clear path to the right of a wall then, later on, to the left of it. Climb a stile then squeeze through a gap in the wall and turn right over the stream. Carry on uphill for 100 yards until you join a farm track. Here you can either turn right to the Setter Dog for refreshments, or turn left and follow the track through the farm with buildings on the left. Ahead, you cross a stream and pass a solitary building, also on the left. Keep left with the wall on your left and, where it turns right, follow the white arrow over a stile to a second arrow pointing out the path uphill and slightly to the left. The route now goes between breeze blocks set into the ground at regular intervals. Cross two stiles and bear right, following the marker. There is a wooden stile to cross in the top right-hand corner of the next field and then the path goes straight ahead, over a farm track and a stone wall stile. After crossing a field and another stile ahead, ford the stream and go forwards along a grass track to the left of a wall. Leave the track when it bears left and go forwards, with the wall on the right, to cross a collapsed wall. Keep going and as you begin to descend the edge of **Lamaload Reservoir** appears on the left. At the bottom of the hill you reach a track by some buildings where you turn right until you come to the road. Turn left along the road back to the car park.

POINTS OF INTEREST:

White Nancy – Monument on top erected, it is believed, to commemorate the Battle of Waterloo. So called because of its colour and after the name of the horse who carried the stone to the summit.

Lamaload Reservoir – Supplies the Macclesfield area. Completed in 1964, with a capacity of 420 million gallons.

REFRESHMENTS:

The Setter Dog, Walker Barn (tel no: 0625 31444). Open daily from 10.30-2.00pm. Serves sandwiches, soups, paté and à la carte meals. Children welcome and dogs allowed into the porch. Outside seating. Willingly accommodates parties of walkers but likes advance notice.

Walk 13 **KNUTSFORD AND TATTON PARK, ROUTE 1** 5m (8km)
Maps: OS Sheets Landranger 109 and 118; Pathfinder SJ 68/78
and SJ 67/77.
*Some cobbled surfaces in Knutsford. Tatton Park is muddy in
parts after wet weather and away from the tarmac surfaces.*
Start: The car park in the centre of Knutsford.

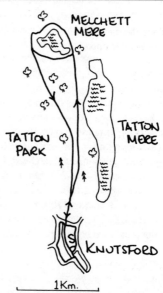

Leave via Malt Street and turn right along King Street, past the **Heritage Centre** on
the left. After 250 yards take a path bearing right into **Tatton Park**, and follow the main
drive for just over 1 mile. Climb the stile on the right of a cattle grid and bear left along
the drive towards Melchett Mere, ignoring the stile on the left. Go ahead a few yards
past a clump of trees and take a grassy path bearing to the left round the mere. Continue
on this path until you reach the gate at the head of the mere. Either keep to the mere bank
back to the main drive or take the grassy path leading off right, to go diagonally over
parkland to join the drive again. Rejoin King Street where you turned off for Tatton
Park and turn left down Drury Lane past the **Ruskin Rooms** and a water tower further
down the hill. Follow the road round to the right along Moorside (noticing the unusual

38

buildings, the work of R H Watt), until it rejoins the far end of King Street near the railway bridge. Turn back again along King Street where there is a group of 17th-century cottages next to the church wall. Go left up Church Hill and turn right into Princess Street. Continue along Princess Street, passing the Methodist Chapel, and turn left through Canute Place and past the White Bear Inn to Gaskell Avenue on the other side of the roundabout. Facing The Heath, where races took place for 200 years, is a row of town houses, including **Heathwaite House** and **Heath House**. Return to Canute Place and go left along Tatton Street in front of the **Lord Eldon** pub. Carry on past some terraced houses and turn right along a short path opposite Drury Lane. Walk right, along King Street, keeping to the right-hand side, to the **Gaskell Memorial Tower**. Return to the car park by the passage opposite.

POINTS OF INTEREST:
The Heritage Centre – Built in the 17th century and now reconstructed.
Tatton Park – A National Trust property owned by the Egerton family until 30 years ago. Park landscaped by Humphry Repton in the late 1700s.
Ruskin Rooms – Built by R H Watt around 1900 as recreation rooms for the laundry workers whose cottages further down the hill he also built.
Heathwaite House – Where Elizabeth Gaskell lived as a child with her Aunt Lumb.
Heath House – The home of Highwayman Higgins who fraternised with the gentry and then robbed them. He was hanged in 1767.
The Lord Eldon – Home of Knutsford's first May Queen crowned in 1864. The landlord changed the name from the Duke of Wellington when the Duke supported the Catholic Emancipation Act.
Gaskell Memorial Tower – The walls are covered with quotations from well-known writers and there is a bust of Mrs Gaskell half-way up the tower.

REFRESHMENTS:
The Royal George, Knutsford (tel no: 0565 4151). Fresh hot and cold meals daily. Children welcome. No dogs.
The White Lion, King Street, Knutsford (tel no: 0565 2018). Cheeses, home-made paté, hot dishes. 12pm-2pm daily. Children welcome. Dogs allowed in garden.

Walk 14   ARLEY AND GREAT BUDWORTH   5 $\frac{1}{2}$m (9km)

Maps: OS Sheets Landranger 109 and 118; Pathfinder SJ 67/77 and SJ 68/78.

A fairly level walk over farmland and through one of Cheshire's loveliest villages. Can be muddy in wet weather.

Start: At 671809, the free car park in Arley.

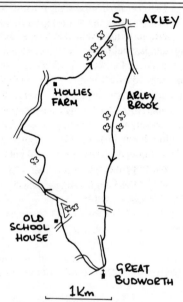

Turn left out of the car park through the gate of Arley Estates, right at the crossroads ahead, and walk on until you reach a sign 'Private, No Through Road'. Turn right, following a signed footpath, and go through a gate keeping left of the field. Cross a stile at the side of a gate, and pass through a small wood. Cross over a footbridge, and Arley Brook and turn left over a stile into a field. Pass through a gate leading on to a well-defined track. Follow this track on to a cement path and go forward to meet a crossing road. Walk forward over the road to enter a field over a small wooden stile in the hedge. With the fence on your right, follow the path to a stile at the far end of a field. Turn right across the field diagonally in the direction of the church ahead and through a gate into Heath Lane. Turn left, cross over the junction ahead and go forward down a gravel track between two bungalows to a facing gate. Turn right of this gate, following a path between trees, passing the schoolhouse on the right with the church on the left to join Church Street opposite the George and Dragon Inn. Turn right along Church Street and bear left down Smithy Lane for 200 yards, arriving at two gates on your right. Take the left-hand gate and follow a signposted route up the field to a gate in a crossing fence. Pass through this gate and turn right then left to skirt the field, keeping a hedge and trees to your right. Near the top of the field the path turns sharp right. With the hedge on your left cross a stile alongside a tree, arriving at a kissing gate. Through this gate go down a lane, taking the lane opposite signposted to Antrobus and Arley. With the old schoolhouse on your left, go to the end of the lane and turn left at the signpost to Antrobus and Warrington. Just before the Antrobus village sign take a footpath to the right along a well-defined track for 200 yards. Passing a small wood on your left, the track goes sharp right. Leave the track and go left into a field keeping a hedge on your left. Turn right at a facing hedge and then, with a fence on the left, pass through a gate just before you reach a small wood. Go through a second gate. The footpath bears right here, but as this field is usually in crop go forward on to Hollins Lane. Turn right and walk for $1/_2$ mile to Hollies Farm. Leaving the lane here, go over a stile into the farm, turn right by a large barn, through a gate and take a facing track, keeping the fence on your left. Walk 100 yards, dropping down to your left, cross over a stile, and across an old footbridge over Arley Brook. Go up the opposite bank, and across a facing field, and a further field, with a hedge on your left. The path, lined with trees and hedgerows, soon emerges on to a track, shortly to meet a crossing lane. Turn left here and return to the starting point of the walk.

REFRESHMENTS:
The George and Dragon (tel no: 0606 891317). 'Olde worlde' pub, serving good food, reasonably priced.

Walk 15　　　　　　**ALDERLEY EDGE**　　　　　5 $\frac{1}{2}$m (9km)

Maps: OS Sheets Landranger 118, Pathfinder SJ 87/97.

A walk through National Trust land, over farmland, with descents and inclines and superb views of the Cheshire Plain.

Start: At 859773, the car park near the Wizard restaurant on the B5087.

Enter a track at the side of the restaurant and follow it straight ahead, passing a National Trust sign on the left and a sign to Edge House Farm on the right. The track shortly turns right, but the way is straight ahead to follow a path through trees with a fence and ditch on the immediate left. The paths drops down with a fence on the right, then enters trees and keeps on down the left of a small gully. At the bottom turn right, cross a stream and climb, passing to the left of outcrops of rock to join a track straight ahead. Follow this track which bears left then right, keep forward descending slightly at first to climb and emerge from trees. The track continues straight ahead, but the walk goes right through an opening in a fence and over a stile to enter a field. Continue with a fence on the right passing a pond, then bear left and cross a stile on the right. Pass over a second stile, then turn left here, climbing uphill, on past a cottage on the right to meet a crossing lane. Turn left, go over a stile at the right-hand side of the entrance gate to Edge House Farm, over a second stile and bear right on to a track. Go over two more stiles and pass a farm. At a crossing road the way is forward, following a path through the trees and turn right at the lane ahead. continue to where the lane turns sharp right. Go down the track leading to Finlow Hill Farm, turn right through a gate just before the farm buildings are reached, then turn left. Keep forward with a fence on the left to cross a stile at the left-hand side of a wood. Skirt around the wood keeping a fence on the right side, then turn left at a crossing fence. Walk on, descending slightly and cross two stiles at the side of Haymans Farm. Go forward with a fence on the left to cross a stile at the side of a facing gate, turn right and proceed along a tree-lined lane past dwellings and forward down a lane. Proceed to the junction with the main road ahead, turn left and continue for $^{1}/_{4}$ mile to arrive at the **Old Mill** of Nether Alderley. Cross the road and follow the sign to the church. Enter the church grounds and pass the old schoolhouse to a stile at the left rear side of the church. Bear right over a stream, and over a stile in a crossing hedge, turn right and proceed to the T-junction ahead where the way is left. After 300 yards turn right on to Bradford Lane, which becomes cobbled and leads to a fork. Turn left here to climb past Bradford House Farm, and Bradford Lodge Nurseries, then next left to the T-junction ahead. Turn left here and cross the road to return to your car.

POINTS OF INTEREST:

The Old Mill – The mill has been restored to its original working order and is well worth a visit.

REFRESHMENTS:

Refreshments are available in a mobile van in the start car park.

Walk 16 KNUTSFORD AND TATTON PARK, ROUTE 2 6m (9.5km)

Maps: OS Sheets Landranger 109 and 118; Pathfinder SJ 67/77 and SJ 68/78.

An easy walk, fairly level through mature woodland and across open parkland. Some paths may be muddy after rain.

Start: At 753787, the car park in the centre of Knutsford.

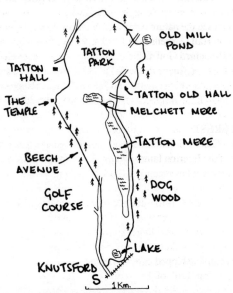

At the rear of the car park is a road adjacent to some parkland. Turn left along this and after 50 yards right on to a footpath beside the edge of a small lake. Just before the footpath goes under a railway, turn left up a rough track past a new housing development and into a wood. Shortly after going around a large fallen tree, turn left over a stile. The path skirts a marshy area thickly strewn with rushes, and then meanders through some beautiful woodland with glimpses of Tatton Mere. Cross a stile in a high fence and then follow the footpath along the shoreline to enter the National Trust property of Tatton Park. After $^1/_2$ mile you will reach a gravel road; follow this to its junction with a metalled road. Turn away from the lake towards some buildings in the trees, and beyond these cross a footbridge over Tatton Brook. Bear right up to a metalled road; on your right is **Tatton Old Hall**. Follow the road around to the right. Beside the fence, next to a children's play area, you will see a wooden platform with a plaque on it. Follow this waymarked trail describing the old manor of Tatton, as far as the old mill pond. Go straight on across a culvert, then bear left along on an intermittent track towards a conifer plantation where the track becomes more distinct and runs parallel to a high deer fence. About $^1/_2$ mile will bring you to a metalled road, the main way into Tatton Park. Turn left along this and follow to a T-junction, where **Tatton Hall and Gardens** are on the right. Keep straight ahead across open parkland towards a thin track which leads through a gate near the edge of Tatton Hall Gardens. On your left you can see the nature reserve of Melchett Mere. Opposite the Temple at the far end of Tatton Hall Gardens is the 'Beech Avenue'. Follow the footpath along this, which skirts Knutsford Golf Course, until you meet a metalled road near to the south entrance of the park. Leave through one of the side gates and after 50 yards turn left along a short footpath which emerges on to King Street in **Knutsford**. Turn left and continue until you reach the road leading down to the car park.

POINTS OF INTEREST:

Tatton Old Hall – This 15th-century building was the home of the lords of the manor, before the arrival of the Egerton family. The oldest part is the Great Hall with its high, carved, quatrefoil roof. It has recently been restored and is open to the public.

Tatton Hall – A grand mansion built in the Neo-classical style for the wealthy Egerton family in 1813. Their extravagantly furnished and decorated rooms are well preserved, as are the servants' quarters which give a fascinating insight into life behind the scenes.

The Gardens – These were laid out in the 1850s and include exotic features, such as a fernery, an orangery, a sunken rose garden and a Japanese garden complete with authentic Shinto Temple, shipped over from Japan.

Knutsford – The 'Cranford' of Elizabeth Gaskell's novel, with several unusual buildings in an Italianate style, designed by R. H. Watt in 1907. They include the Ruskin Rooms and the Gaskell Memorial Tower. (See Walk 13.)

REFRESHMENTS:
Tatton Park (tel no: 0565 54822).
The White Lion, Knutsford (tel no: 0565 2018).
The Rose and Crown Hotel, Knutsford (tel no: 0565 52366).
Patisserie, Knutsford (tel no: 0565 2669).

Walk 17 **WILDBOARCLOUGH TO THREE SHIRES HEAD** 6m (9.5km)

Maps: OS Landranger Sheet 118 & 119; Outdoor Leisure 24.

A gritstone walk near to the source of the River Dane with some delightful picnic spots and swimming holes.

Start: At 987699, the Peak National Park car park at Clough House.

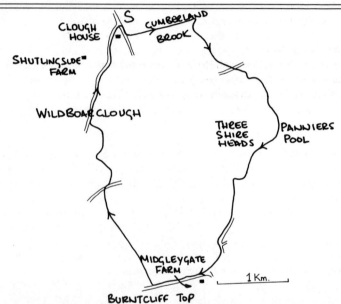

Follow a broad track by Clough House signposted to the Cat and Fiddle Inn up Cumberland Brook. Keep the woodland on your right, and just past the end of the woodland go right on another track; this is Footpath No.103 of the Peak Footpath Preservation Society. Follow this for $^1/_2$ mile until you meet the main Buxton road. Go directly across the road and over a stile in the corner of the field on the left, and continue down over several fields to meet the River Dane in its infancy. Follow the true right bank (Cheshire) of the river to the Pack Horse Bridge and Panniers Pool at Three Shires Head. This is where Derbyshire, Staffordshire and Cheshire meet. Follow the sandy track up right and away from the river for $^1/_4$ mile until it is possible to cut down left across fields to reach Knar Farm. Follow the gated metalled road for $^3/_4$ mile to meet

46

a road. Go right here past Midgleygate Farm and over Burnt Cliff Top to the Eagle and Child Farm on the right. A track leads right here across open country for about 1 mile to reach the main Buxton road. Turn right here past a gate to a stile on the left. Go over this stile and head diagonally right to a lone barn. Turn left at the barn to the top right of a wood, cross over a stile and into a disused lane at the left side of the next wood. Go down this lane and diagonally left to another short lane. Turn left here for 100 metres then cross over a stile into a wood. Carry on down through the woods to cross a footbridge over Clough Brook just by the Crag Inn. Turn right here and walk along the road for $^1/_2$ mile to regain the start point at Clough House.

REFRESHMENTS:

Midgleygate Farm. Teas with Hovis, to which children are welcome. Dogs are not, because there are farm dogs about.

The Crag Inn, Wildboarclough (tel no: 0260 227239).

Walk 18   NORTH RODE AND GAWSWORTH   6m (9.5km)

Maps: OS Sheets Landranger 118; Pathfinder SJ 86/89.

Leafy lanes, canal paths, woodlands and a lake.

Start: At 889665, the car park behind North Rode village hall.

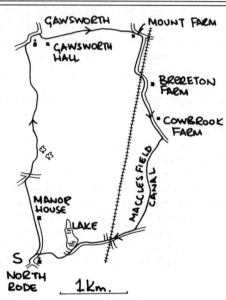

On leaving the car park go left, passing a cottage on your right and going through a facing gateway. Fork left, crossing over a cattle grid to arrive at a sign saying 'No Through Road'. Continue down a concrete lane climbing to pass a farmhouse on your right, and go over a double stile at the side of a facing gate. Carry on over a field passing to the left-hand side of a small wood and follow a well-defined track. Continue with a fence on your left, on a stony track which becomes grassy, to cross a stile at the side of a gate. Go right for a short way along Pexall Road , and go straight on at the junction ahead to cross a stile at the side of a facing gate. Go forward with a fence on your left and climb slightly to cross two fields over stiles. After the second stile go straight over a rough crossing track, then down a tree-lined track for 50 yards, and over a stile at the side of a gate. Keep forward here with a hedge on your left, and cross a stile in a fence one field's length away.

48

Gawsworth Church can be seen in the distance at this point. Keep forward in the direction of this church, and cross a stile. The next stile is at the right-hand corner of the field, so skirt this field to cross it. Now walk 30 yards up a track to cross a stile on your right, cross the next field to a stile in the left-hand corner, and continue over two more stiles to the field just before the church. The path bears slightly left to skirt the edge of the field, and you then descend wooden steps to enter a lane. Turn right, continue walking up the lane and pass the **Parish Church of St James** and two ponds on your right. Go right into the entrance lane of the hall, then left to pass the entrance gate. Carry straight on to pass a statue on your left, then, after passing Gawsworth Court, walk down a gravel track to a gate. Keep forward with a hedge on your right, and cross four fields to arrive at a crossing lane.

Turn right and go past Mount Farm, then right again just before a railway bridge and go down Cowbrook Lane. This takes you over a railway then drops down over Cow Brook to climb through trees.

The lane now approaches a bridge over the canal. Do not go over this bridge, but go through a gap on the left to drop down on to the canal towpath. Turn right under the bridge, and continue under bridges 52 and 53, arriving at Bosley Locks. Leave the canal towpath at the side of bridge 54 and turn right to follow a lane. Shortly the lane turns sharp right after passing over the railway, but this walk goes straight ahead through lodge gates where a sign reads 'Private Road to the Manor House – North Rode'. Go forward and after $^1/_4$ mile the lane skirts the edge of a lake. Keep forward now and turn left just before a cattle grid. Pass through a gate and cross a field along a tree-lined grassy track to a facing gate. Go through this gate and enter the lane ahead, which leads you back to your car.

POINTS OF INTEREST:
The Parish Church of St James – Well worth a visit on this walk, the church stands on the site of a Norman chapel. The walls and roof are over 500 years old. The Fitton family tombs can be seen inside the church and the old tomb dates back to 1608. A leaflet describing points of interest to visitors can be obtained in the church.

Walk 19 **REDESMERE** 6m (9.5km)

Maps: OS Sheets Landranger 118, Pathfinder SJ 87/97 & 86/96.
An easy walk over farmlands, down lanes and round a mere.
Start: At 850715, near the head of Redesmere.

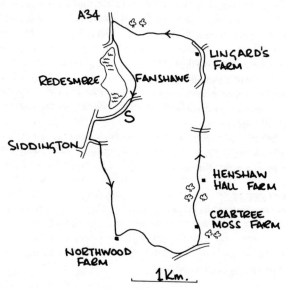

Walk back to the main road and turn left and then left again, with **Siddington Church** on your right. Walk up the drive to the church, go down a path facing the porch and enter a field through a gate. Go straight ahead and cross three fields and three stiles. After crossing the third stile descend slightly with a fence on your right, and cross a stile by a pond. Continue with a grassy bank on your left to arrive at a stile on your left, walking in the direction of Northwood Farm. With a fence on your left, just before the farm gate, cross a stile. The way now is forward and then right, skirting the farm to join a well-defined track which continues for $^3/_4$ mile, passing four gates. Go left at a crossing lane, and after $^1/_4$ mile take the track just before a wood on the left, where there is a signboard indicating Crabtree Moss Farm. Proceed through the farmyard, pass through a facing gate, continue for a short distance down an overgrown lane, then turn right along a well-defined track through two gates. Turn right to pass between the outbuildings of

Henshaw Hall Farm. Keep forward along a gravel track which leads into a lane and shortly meets a crossing lane. Go straight across, and then through a gate in the opposite hedge to climb steadily along a gravel track. Pass dwellings on the left and go through a facing gate, then continue with trees on both sides to pass through a further gate into a large sloping field. Keep forward and descend to a crossing fence straight ahead. Go over a stile then cross a bridge over Fanshaw Brook. Climb over a stile into a field, keeping the hedge to your left and farm buildings to your right. Cross a stile with a cattle grid to your right; the road is straight ahead passing cottages on your left and a joining lane on the right. Keep forward to arrive at a farm on the left where Henbury Moss post box is let into a stone wall. Leave the lane and pass by the farm buildings and through a gate at the right side of a barn. Keep forward along a rough track and go through a gate which leads into a fenced dirt track. Keep straight ahead past a small farm on the right, to emerge on the main road opposite the entrance to Capesthorne Hall. Turn left and, where the road bends right, bear left through a gate walking along the eastern shore of Redesmere. Pass the Yacht Club and go through a gate to follow a path through trees. The lane bears left but you cross a stile directly ahead into a field keeping Redesmere Lake and trees to your right. Turn right at a facing lane back to your car.

POINTS OF INTEREST:
Siddington Church – Consecrated in 1521, consists of a black and white timber frame, with wattle and daub filling.

REFRESHMENTS:
There is usually a mobile snack bar in this area.

Walk 20   PLUMLEY AND HOLFORD HALL   6m (9.5km)

Maps: OS Sheets Landranger 118; Pathfinder SJ 67/77.
An easy walk, fairly level through farmland and woodland.
Start: At 722754, Plumley Station car park.

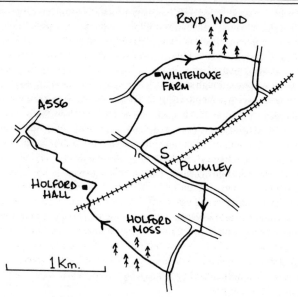

Leave the station car park by some steps up to the road, and turn left across the railway bridge, passing The Golden Pheasant Inn. After 300 yards turn right over a stile. Initially the footpath skirts a plantation, then crosses a stile and follows a hedge to your left. Cross a stile and footbridge and after skirting a pond, keep left beside the hedge, reaching a metalled road through a white gate. Turn right and then left into Cheadle Lane. After $^1/_4$ mile, take a footpath on your right over a cattle grid, along an ICI access road. Keep right at a junction, passing through a short stretch of woodland. The track becomes much rougher, and you keep straight ahead. Just before another cattle grid, turn off to the right beside a hedge, then cross a stile and keep left, eventually taking a footpath between high hedges up to a railway bridge. Cross over and on the other side take a path across the field to the gateway opposite. Turn right beside a hedge and follow the path to its junction with a wide track. Turn left along this track and follow to another junction. Bear right here through a gate, passing through the farmyard of **Holford Hall**, and at the end of the driveway, cross a bridge over Peover Eye. The road beyond leads up through Holford Farm to the A556. Turn right here along the grass verge and after 100 yards take a footpath on your right, across the stile, beside the right-hand gate. Now follow the hedge on your left, crossing two more stiles, and then go straight ahead across a field to another stile. Bear left here towards a gateway with some houses beyond. Cross a stile and make for these houses, emerging on to a metalled road, through a gate in the corner of the field. Take the footpath opposite and keep straight on, following the hedge to your right. Cross two stiles, then turn left to reach the farm road leading to Whitehouse Farm. Turn right along this into the farmyard, and beyond the farm buildings pass through some wide red gates. Cross a small bridge over a brook to reach the edge of Royd Wood, and turn right along the wood, keeping beside it for about $^1/_2$ mile. Where the wood edge turns to the left, keep straight ahead across a field, emerging on to a metalled road, over a stile. Turn right here past a thatched cottage and where the road bends to the left, take a footpath on your right. Go through a gate and turn left along a hedge to reach steps leading to a railway crossing. Do not cross, but turn right alongside the railway embankment. Follow this across 2 stiles and when you reach another railway crossing, turn right away from the railway. Soon you will reach a gateway. Go through this and turn right along the opposite side of the hedge. When you approach another gateway, bear left across the field to a gap in the hedge, with a plank footbridge on the other side. Cross this and continue straight on beside the hedge, crossing a further stile. When you reach the edge of Plumley, turn left over a stile into a garden and then immediately right into a passage which skirts several back gardens. Soon you will reach the main village road, near the Post Office. Turn left along this to return to the station car park.

POINTS OF INTEREST:
Holford Hall – A beautiful black and white timbered house surrounded by a moat, built for Lady Mary Cholmondeley in 1601. She was famous for her law suits, one of which lasted 40 years. Nearby, where the bridge crosses Peover Eye, are the remains of an old watermill.

REFRESHMENTS:
The Golden Pheasant Hotel, Plumley (tel no: 056 581 2261).

Walks 21 & 22 CIRCUIT OF SHUTLINGSLOE 6m (9.5km) or 12m (19km)

Maps: OS Sheets Landranger 118; Outdoor Leisure 24.

A stunning walk around and over Shutlingsloe Moor.

Start: At 982687, by the bridge in Wildboarclough.

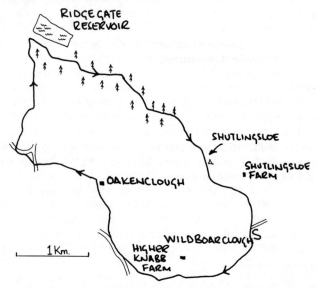

Walk away from Wildboarclough south to the Crag public house. At a footpath sign go over a stone stile and contour the hillside over stiles, with Shutlingsloe on your right and fine views across the Cloughbrook Valley to your left. Go through a gate below Higher Knabb Farm and diagonally right to meet a walled green lane. Follow this left to the road. Go down 150 metres to the stream bridge and follow a track and stream right to a stone footbridge. Go over this and left up Oakenclough valley to the magnificent farm. Pass this on its left. Go left up the hill over stiles, and past a tarn to exit at the Haning Gate Inn. Go through the pub yard and down the footpath to a road. Go left for 100 yards then right on to the Gritstone Trail. Follow the Trail to a large farm and go through the farmyard and straight up the hillside past a wooden house. Go over stiles and a small road, then over more stiles to a farm.

Go left at the farm for 100 yards, then right over a stile. Just past a house leave the Gritstone Trail and cut down right into the wood by way of a footbridge and stile. Climb a hill in the wood. At the wood edge, just before the reservoir, there is a sign for Shutlingsloe Forest Trail No. 3. Take this footpath along well marked tracks. After about $1^1/_4$ miles go over a stile on to open moorland. Follow the waymarked and repaired track to the mountainous Shutlingsloe. Climb this and descend the east side to Shutlingsloe Farm and a lane. Take the lane down right until you meet a road. Turn left to the start point.

This walk can be combined with walk No. 17 Wildboarclough to Three Shires Head for a long and interesting gritstone day.

REFRESHMENTS:
The Crag Inn, Wildboarclough (tel no: 0260 227239). Lunches and evening meals. Outside eating area. Children welcome. No dogs inside.
Brookside Restaurant, Wildboarclough (tel no: 0260 227632). 200 yards beyond the Crag Inn. Grills, snacks, teas, licensed. Children welcome, dogs not allowed.
The Hanging Gate, Haddon, Sutton (tel no: 02605 2238). Food lunch and evening. Outside eating. Children welcome. Dogs not allowed.

Walk 23 THE PEOVER ROUND 6½m (10km)

Maps: OS Sheets Landranger 118; Pathfinder SJ 67/77.

A walk through flat countryside, visiting two unusual churches.
Start: At 764747, in the lay-by on the A50 2 miles south of
Knutsford.

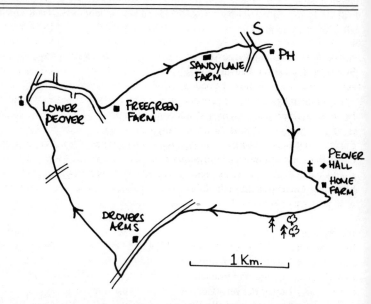

Walk on along the road for ½ mile to a junction and sharp bend. Continue alongside
the Lodge by the Whipping Stocks Inn going through two gates. Follow the track
through what was, in Medieval times, a fine hunting park. Cross the stream, then leave
the main track and bear right along a grass track towards the square church tower seen
ahead. Follow the fence on the right to a facing stone wall. On the left is Peover Hall,
an Elizabethan Manor House. Go over a rough wooden stile, then through the wood
among rhododendrons. You will shortly arrive at **St Lawrence, Over Peover**.

After visiting the church, turn left past the outbuildings and stables of Home Farm
to a lane. Turn right and continue past St Anthony's Cottages. The lane becomes a
track but you go straight on into the wood when the track bears sharp left. The woodland
path soon becomes a track with the remains of a conifer plantation on the left. Join a

lane by the greenhouses of Long Lane Nurseries and follow this to the main road. Bear left and follow the A50, crossing a bridge over the Peover Eye stream continuing to the Drovers Arms on the right. This is a good place to stop for a meal and accepts children and dogs. From the Drovers Arms it is best to continue along the road for 300 yards. Go through a gate on the right and follow the track across a field. Go through a second gate and on to a third on the other side of the field. Cross a stile here, then go over the facing stile and bear left along the hedge and fence. Cross three more stiles and at the third stile bear right along the fence to another stile. Cross this and bear left with the Peover Eye beneath you on the right. Follow the stream, crossing a number of stiles. Shortly after crossing a lane you will reach a powerful weir. Ahead, you will see **St Oswald's, Lower Peover**, a striking building of black and white timber with a square stone tower. Follow the path up to the church.

The churchyard has a gate connecting it directly to the Bells of Peover Inn behind. From the Inn, continue past the fish pond in the car park. Go over the bridge and turn right at the junction. Bear right at the next junction along Free Green Lane. Opposite Free Green Cottage leave the lane and go left up the bridleway which leads past Free Green Farm. Go through the farmyard and continue along the track through a gate. At a second gate bear right. Walk to Sandy Lane Farm, then through its yard, which can be muddy. Go on past the outbuildings to a road. Turn left and follow the road a short distance back to your car.

POINTS OF INTEREST:

St Lawrence, Over Peover – Begun in 1400 by the Mainwarings, the chapel contains Medieval marble effigies of family members. During the Civil War the Mainwarings took Parliament's side and Roundhead soldiers were billeted in the church.

St Oswald's, Lower Peover – Contains a fine timber ceiling and Jacobean box pews. Begun in 1269, it holds six bells, the original two of which were made in 1546.

REFRESHMENTS:

The Drovers Arms (tel no: 056 581 2255). A friendly inn serving a good range of home cooked meals, reasonably priced.

The Bells of Peover (tel no: 056 581 2269). A traditional inn in a picturesque setting, serving high quality food.

Walk 24 and 25   **ADLINGTON**   6^1/$_2$m (10 km) or 7^1/$_2$m (12km)
Maps: OS Sheets Landranger 109 and 118; Pathfinder SJ 87/97 and SJ 88/98.

An easy walk through fields, woods and along the canal towpath.
Start: At 912806, the lay-by on the A523 just north of Legh Arms.

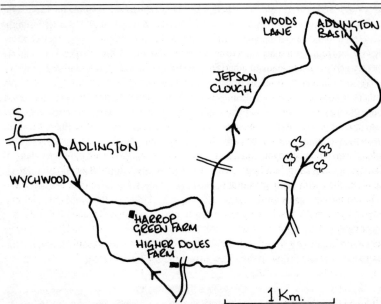

Leave the car park in the direction of the Legh Arms, turn left into Brookledge Lane at the crossroads and continue for 350 yards to turn right into Wych Lane. Where the lane goes right continue on a track at the edge of Wych Wood. Where the track bends right go over a stile, cross a field to Harrop Green Farm and then go over a waymarked stile to a track. Follow the track left to another waymarked stile. Go over and cross the field beyond diagonally to a stile by a single oak tree and a group of trees. Cross the next field, to the top left corner and a stile. Cross the footpath and the cycle track beyond and follow the sign for the canal over a further stile. Follow a path to the right of a wood to a stile at the far end. Do not go over **Macclesfield Canal** bridge ahead but take the steps on the left down to the towpath.

Go left, under bridge 21, then, 100 yards beyond, crossing the waymarked stile on the left. Bear right, going right of and behind a small pool, then left to a stile in the trees. Go over and right to a second stile by a gate and over on to a road. Almost opposite is a stile on to a track signed 'Jepson Clough'. Go over another stile, and down towards a house. Go right following a white arrow and skirt the house to a stile. Here, join a path which crosses a stream, goes over a stile and uphill to another, left of a farm. Go over on to a tarmac drive. Turn left, fork right and continue over the canal bridge and through a caravan site to Wood End Farm where a gate bars the way. Take a path on the left and go over a series of stiles with the canal on your left to reach Adlington Basin. Go right and, after about 700 yards, leave the track when it bends right and go over two stiles ahead into a field. Turn sharp right to another stile and then half-left to the far hedgerow where a gap by a gate leads to a hedged-in track. Follow this to a road. Go right for nearly $^3/_4$ mile then bear left to Bollington and, at the public footpath sign 200 yards further on, turn right over a stile and then head left and downhill towards Styperson Pool. Cross a stile to enter woodlands following a path left of a pool to join a drive and then a road. Go left for 225 yards and then follow a Public Footpath sign on the right just before a cottage. Cross the canal bridge and go right, then left, towards Higher Doles Farm. Go over a cycle track and footpath and through a gate opposite. Shortly, turn left passing farm buildings on the right and follow a rough track to a house, Oakdene. Stay with the track keeping Oakdene on your right. Go over several cattle grids and through gates until, just before a house, you turn left off the track. With a hedge on your right, reach and go over a stile next to a hedge gap and then under the power cables. Turn right and keep to the left of a hedge to cross a stile. Turn left and cross a footbridge and stile ahead. Go right and, keeping to the edge of the field, cross a stile. Bear left and follow a path to a stile on to a farm track. Turn right to Wych Lane and the route back to the start.

POINTS OF INTEREST:
The Macclesfield Canal – Opened in 1831, the canal is $26^1/_2$ miles long and was designed by Thomas Telford. It connects the Peak Forest and Trent and Mersey Canals.

REFRESHMENTS:
The Legh Arms, Adlington (tel no: 0625 829212). Serves bar meals, light meals and a few vegetarian dishes. Children welcome. Dogs at the manager's discretion.
Adlington Hall (tel no: 0625 829206). Serves teas and refreshments from 3.00-5.30pm when the Hall is open.

Walk 26 JENKIN CHAPEL AND WINDGATHER ROCKS 7m (11km)
Maps: OS Sheets Landranger 118; Pathfinder SJ 87/97.
Quite a strenuous walk on good paths with fine views.
Start: At 995778, the forest car park at Pym Chair.

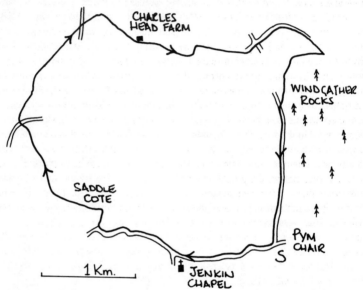

Leave the car park and turn left to a T-junction. Turn right, towards Rainow, and walk as far as **Jenkin Chapel.** Here, where the road bends sharp left, continue ahead down a minor road, cobbled in places. Go down and then uphill for $^3/_4$ mile until, after passing a wood on your left, the road begins to flatten out. Go over a stile with a yellow way mark, on the right. Go ahead to another stile and turn sharp left on the other side, proceeding with a wall and a wire fence on the immediate left. Ignore the first stile in the fence but cross a rickety one ahead and go down to Moss Brook. Turn right. Do not cross the brook here, crossing instead just before a wall joins it from the left. Cross a stile ahead and go over a smaller brook on stepping stones continuing uphill with a wall on your left. Go through a boggy patch to two stiles. Take the left one and carry on with a wall and a fence on the right. Cross a stile on to a farm track and, with farm buildings on your left, go ahead to join a main road. Opposite there is a gap in the fence leading to a stile. Go over and bear left to cross another stile. Go sharp right over a stile adjacent to a metal gate and follow a track downhill to Black Brook. Cross a stile and go over the brook, continuing uphill to cross a further stile. Turn right with the wall on your left and after 25 yards fork right and walk through an avenue of trees to a main road. Cross and continue straight ahead up the track opposite. From this point you can see Whaley Moor and Kinder Scout to the left, if the day is clear.

At Charles Head Farm go straight on with the farm buildings on the right, then, a little further on, bear right and follow a rough track downhill to a stile. Go over and down, passing to the left of a small stone building to reach a footbridge over Todd Brook. On the far side bear left up a track towards an old house. Just past this turn left, go through an iron gate and straight on towards the next house. Go through another gate, then sharp right up a track between the house and an out-house. Go on through gates and fields towards some farm buildings to the left of Windgather Rocks, and exit on to a minor road via a stone stile. Turn left. At a junction of roads continue straight across and fork right up a waymarked track shortly afterwards. Pass a house on your left and go ahead with a wall on your right. Keep to the left of a solitary beech tree and continue with the wall on your immediate right. When the wall bends to the right keep straight on over a stile, then go sharp right over another stile into a wood. Just before going in to the wood there is an excellent view of the Goyt Valley if you walk on a short way. The path through the wood follows a wall on the right. Keep with it as it turns left and go over a stile. When the wall bends sharp right follow it to cross a further stile. Walk left along the top of Windgather Rocks and follow the track which will take you back to your car.

POINTS OF INTEREST:

Jenkin Chapel – Built by a group of farmers in the late 18th century. A simple altar is formed from planks of wood roughly nailed together. There is a plaster rosette in the ceiling, a round window of modern stained glass and a chimney stack.

REFRESHMENTS:

The Bull's Head, Kettleshulme (tel no: 066 33 733225).
The Robin Hood Inn, Church Lane, Rainow (tel no: 0625 74060).

Walk 27   LAMALOAD AND SHINING TOR   7m (11km)

Maps: OS Sheets Landranger 118; Pathfinder SJ 87/97.

A fairly strenuous walk on good paths.

Start: At 976753, the car park on the east side of Lamaload
Reservoir.

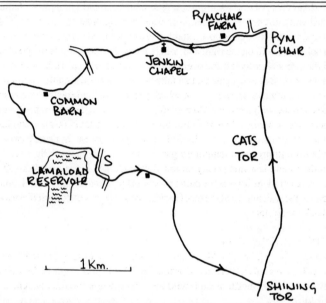

Leave the car park by the main entrance, turn right and after 400 yards, at the bridge
over the stream, turn left, signed 'Burbage via Shining Tor'. Go over a stile. Stay with
the grassy path by the stream to reach another stile. Go over and ahead, away from the
stream, passing the ruin of Eaves Farm on the left. Cross a stile and go up to a gap in
the wall ahead. Windgather Rocks are on the left skyline. Bear right and follow the track
to join a wall coming downhill on the right. At this point the path levels out and bends
to the right. The views to the south are to Shutlingsloe and Sutton Common Radio Mast.

Keeping the wall on your right, go between two standing stones and, after the path
and wall bend to the left, cross a stile and go straight up to the ridge. Turn right at the
ridge having crossed a stile and follow the path to the summit of **Shining Tor** which
is gained by crossing a ladder stile.

Retrace your steps and continue along the ridge, with the Goyt Valley on your right, passing Cat's Tor on your way. Turn left at the end of the ridge on to a road and proceed in the Rainow direction as far as Jenkin Chapel (see Walk 25). From the chapel, take the path to Rainow, as signed near a stile almost opposite the entrance. Head away from the chapel towards a barn at the bottom of the hill and cross an inconspicuous stone stile 50 yards before the wall corner. Cross the footbridge ahead. Turn right and ford the stream further on, to the left of a barn. Continue uphill with, first of all, a wall, then a 'hedge', on your left. Go over a stile and bear slightly right to another stile by a gate. Go over into a wood. Follow a track through the wood, emerging over a stile. Keep ahead with a wall on the right and, where the wall turns sharp right, go ahead over one stile and then slightly left and over another to join a road. Turn left and 150 yards further on turn right through a gate on to a farm track which is the public footpath to Rainow. Pass behind the farmhouse, from which point Lamaload Reservoir comes into view, and continue with a low wall to the left. Cross a stile and bear left to cross another. Go ahead over a stone stile into Common Barn farmyard. Go through the farmyard to a 'stile' at the junction of two walls. Still keeping the wall on the right, cross a further stile and turn left through a temporary gate 75 yards on to join a farm track. By a ruined building there is a stile giving on to a downhill, well-worn path to the Water Works below. Behind the houses the path crosses a stile. Turn half-left uphill, and go through a gap in the wall almost at the top. Go right to join a track on the left of a wall and follow it back to the start.

POINTS OF INTEREST:
Shining Tor – 559m (1,834ft) high. The ridge from Shining Tor to Pym Chair marks the county boundary between Cheshire and Derbyshire, and is the highest point in Cheshire. To the north are the wild and extensive moorlands of Kinder Scout and Bleaklow.

REFRESHMENTS:
The Setter Dog, Walker Barn (tel no: 0625 31444).
The Highwayman, Rainow (tel no: 0625 734245). $1^1/_2$ miles north-east of Rainow on A5002 to Whaley Bridge.

Walk 28   **AROUND LYME PARK**   8m (13km)

Maps: OS Sheets Landranger 109; Pathfinder SJ 88/98.

A pleasant ramble around Lyme Park.

Start: At 974847, Fountain Square, Disley.

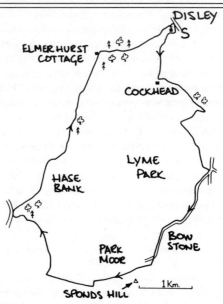

Turn up Ringobells Lane, by the side of the White Horse and climb the hill. Turn right in front of the Quaker Meeting House, cross a bridge and go up steps towards the church. Immediately beyond the cemetery, go left over a stile and cross the field to a gate in the far corner. Turn left on to a lane. Shortly turn right into the corner of a field and cross to the opposite corner. Rejoin the lane, and follow it to Cockhead Farm. Just before the lane turns into the farm, go over a stile on the left. Follow the path, which becomes a good track, through woods to a lane opposite Drake Carr Cottage.

      Turn right and just before Lyme Park's East Lodge go over a stile, left, signposted to Kettleshulme. Cross the field, aiming left of a telegraph pole, and follow a faint path which passes above a line of trees as it crosses the next field. An even fainter track around the hillside leads to a gate. Go through, bear left to cross a stream and then head for a stile by a gate. Go over and turn right. Follow the right edge of the field to a farm.

Enter the farmyard by a stile and leave by the lane. On reaching a road, turn right up a lane signposted for Bowstonegate. After crossing a stile you are on the Gritstone Trail for a while, on a track up Sponds Hill. When the good stone wall on your right suddenly bears right, follow it, shortly crossing a stile. Where the new path bears left, keep to the wall again to reach a stile in a fence. Turn left along the fence until a second stile is reached. Turn right here, to follow a high crumbling stone wall downhill.

Just beyond a stand of fir trees, turn right on to a farm track. Turn left over a stile after a short distance, and follow a grassy path leading over the brow to the left of a farm. Cross a stream and follow a path round a bend. Keep right to follow the wall to a stile. Over the stile, keep to the right passing a small cottage in a hollow and eventually reaching a farmhouse. Go over a stile by a gate and follow a lane down to the Methodist Church, Green Close, Shrigley. Turn sharp right round the front of the church to follow a narrow lane past the West Gate of **Lyme Park**.

Just beyond West Park Gate Farm, go over a ladder stile and follow a stony path past the sheep dip and around the left side of the hill. After crossing a deer fence into the park, **Lyme Cage** can be seen.

Just before the stony track becomes a metalled road, turn sharp left across a field to a ladder stile. Over the stile, keep to the right edge of the fields. After a gate, then a stile, continue to a gate at the edge of Platt Wood. Bear left down to a collection of three gates on the farm road. Take the middle gate and follow the wall until it bends left, then head upwards to a stile on the hilltop. Cross it and carry on down the hill, heading for the far right corner of the field. Here, two gates lead around the back of Elmerhurst Cottage on to the lane. Climb a stile by a large gate and follow the lane past two cottages to the park road. On the far side of the road, squeeze through a narrow iron gate to the left of the North Lodge and follow the lane to a fork. Bear left, back to the start.

POINTS OF INTEREST:

Lyme Park – The Hall is a National Trust property, set in 1,300 acres of deer park and formal gardens. It was the home of the Legh family for 600 years and is a blend of Elizabethan, Georgian and Regency architecture.

Lyme Cage – Built on the highest point of the park in the 16th century by Sir Peter Legh V. Its four towers are a prominent landmark for miles around.

REFRESHMENTS:

Disley boasts a good variety of pubs, some serving food. Refreshments are also available in the park at the car park kiosk and in the Servants Hall Tearoom (tel no: 0663 62033).

Walk 29   **KETTLESHULME AND SHINING TOR**   9m (14.5km)
Maps: OS Sheets Landranger 118; Outdoor Leisure 24.
A fairly strenuous walk, along a secluded valley and a high ridge.
Start:At 976753, the car park at the northern end of the Lamaload
Reservoir.

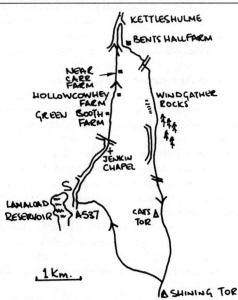

Turn left out of the car park and at the junction turn right. Follow the road to a T-junction
and Jenkin Chapel (see Walk 26). Take the footpath opposite, on the left. Cross a stile
and bear slightly left to pass through a gateway, before descending to Green Booth
Farm in the Todd Brook Valley. Go around the farm to the right between some derelict
buildings, then over a stile next to a gate. Follow the track beyond around to the right
and through another gate to reach Hollowcowhey Farm. Pass this on the left and then
head straight across the field beyond to a gate. Go through this and follow the fence to
a stile above a footbridge. Go over and take a path on the other side up to a disused
cottage. Turn left over a stile and keep ahead over further stiles to reach Near Carr Farm.
Go through a gate into the farmyard and follow a rough track past the farmhouse and
then through the farmyards of Neighbourway and Thorneycroft to reach a metalled

road. Turn left and go down to the A5002 where a right turn will take you into Kettleshulme. Ahead are the Bulls Head and the Swan Inn. Go right into an alley behind the Swan Inn and climb steps to a road above. Turn right and after crossing a stream take a footpath on the left along the driveway to Bents Hall Farm. Go past the farm and just short of some more buildings bear left over a stile and down to a stream. Follow the footpath along the left bank to reach a metalled road. Turn right and after 50 yards take a footpath on your left. Head diagonally right to a stile in the field corner. Pass left of a broken wall and after crossing stiles and gates in front of a farmhouse, turn left on to a farm track and go through a gate by the farmhouse. A little beyond this turn right through a gateway and then climb beside a wall up to **Windgather Rocks** which can be seen ahead.

At the other end of the escarpment, a step-stile leads to a footpath which runs parallel to a road. Follow this for $^1/_2$ mile to a stile. Do not go over, but bear diagonally left along a fence. This footpath climbs through moorland to stiles emerging on to a road. Opposite, a broad path leads up into open country. This is the splendid ridge walk between Cats Tor and Shining Tor (see Walk 27), a distance of 2 miles. The views here are extensive. From Shining Tor retrace your steps 100 yards and turn left over a stile, descending steeply beside a wall. Beyond a depression in the ridge, the path levels out somewhat for about $^1/_2$ mile before plunging steeply again, crossing several stiles to reach the valley below. In the valley bottom bear left down the right bank of the stream to reach a road above Lamaload Reservoir. Turn right along this, to return to the car park.

POINTS OF INTEREST:
Windgather Rocks – One of the best known crags in the Peak District among rock climbers. A particular favourite of those new to the sport.

REFRESHMENTS:
The Bulls Head, Kettleshulme (tel no: 066 33 3225).
The Swan Inn, Kettleshulme (tel no: 066 33 2943).

Maps: OS Sheets Landranger 117; Pathfinder SJ 27/37.
A pleasant walk through woodlands, near a delightful village.
Start: At 318739, a small parking area near the school in Burton.

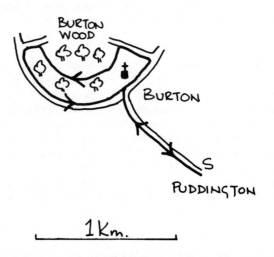

Walk back up Puddington Lane to the centre of the village. Go right at the top of the lane and pass the church entrance on your left. Continue past the library on the right and you will shortly arrive at Vicarage Lane on the left. Walk down the lane for 200 yards to reach a kissing gate on your left. Go through and take a narrow path between trees. The path descends and leads down facing steps here to **Burton Church**. Give yourself time to stop and look around here at this interesting old church.

Retrace the route, going up the steps. Go left along level ground, on a well-defined track passing a Quaker burial ground on the right. Keep to the track until you reach a facing fence. Go through a gap in the fence and take a well-defined track through woods. Continue with railings on your immediate left, then bearing left where the path forks. Follow the path into a gully to reach a kissing gate. Go through on to a road. Go left, crossing the road, to follow a tree-lined pavement. Descend steps, then go left into

Burton. Shortly you pass the gates of Burton Manor on your right, and then reach Burton Post Office. Turn next right to enter Puddington Lane which takes you back to your car.

POINTS OF INTEREST:

Burton Church – The clock was installed in 1751 and is a most unusual time piece. It has one hand, and the hours are divided into four divisions, with each division representing 15 minutes. The church contains Saxon relics found during excavation on the site.

Walk 31   **WALTON**   3m (5km)

Maps: OS Sheets Landranger 108; Pathfinder SJ 48/58 & 68/78.

A pleasant walk along a canal path and country lanes.

Start: At 597852, the Walton Hall Garden car park, Higher
Walton.

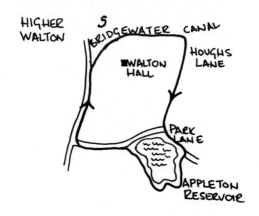

Leave the car park and descend to the **Walton Stretch** of the Bridgewater Canal (see
also Walk 9), via wooden steps. Go left along the canal towpath, under a bridge, then
left away from the towpath. Go left again and over the bridge. Go down Hough Lane,
passing Beech Tree Farm, then Hillfoot Farm. Soon Walton Golf Course is on both
sides, but stay on the lane to reach Appleton Reservoir. Go left there, down Park Lane.
At the end of the reservoir climb steps to reach a well-defined track that skirts the
reservoir, arriving once again on Park Lane.

Go left past dwellings and the golf course on your right to arrive at a crossroads.
Go right down Warrington Road, passing the main entrance to Walton Golf Course to
reach a canal bridge. At a crossing road go right past the Walton Arms on the left. Keep
right and go down a 'No Through Road' back to **Walton Gardens** and your car.

POINTS OF INTEREST:

The Walton Stretch – This section of the Bridgewater Canal was not opened until 1776 after an Act of Parliament forced the landowner to allow the Duke of Bridgewater's engineer Brindley to complete the work.

Walton Gardens – Opened to the public in 1945 and well worth a visit. The grounds are open from dawn to dusk every day of the year.

REFRESHMENTS:

Refreshments and toilets are available at Walton Gardens.

Walk 32 HALE VILLAGE AND THE MERSEY SHORE 3m (5km)
Maps: OS Sheets Landranger 108; Pathfinder SJ 48/58.
An easy walk on good surfaced footpaths.
Start:At 469825, the car park near the new stores in Hale.

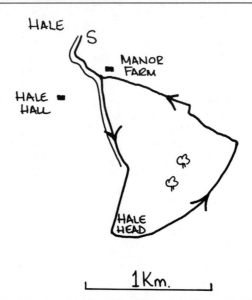

Turn right from the car park and walk for 100 yards before turning left as the road forks to a traffic island. Go down the lane for another 100 yards to the Childe of Hale inn, a favourite with walkers who enjoy a 'log fire' atmosphere.

Beyond the Childe of Hale the road splits into two. Take the right-hand fork into Church End. After 200 yards take Church Road and follow it to **St Mary's Church** on your right. Pass the church and continue for a further $^1/_2$ mile through a landscape of agricultural farmland. On reaching a gateway pass through a pinch gap to the right and take a footpath to **Hale Lighthouse** about 600 yards away.

A Right of Way signpost directs you on to the Mersey Way, a newly established long distance footpath network, which you follow for the next $^3/_4$ mile. The footpath follows the contours of the Mersey Estuary and stands high on a bank above areas of saltmarsh rich in wildlife. A Right of Way sign directs you from the footpath to two pinch gaps on the right. Turn inland back on to Within Way and follow the lane for the next mile back into the village of Hale. It emerges in Church Road, opposite the large Manor House where the poet John Betjemen stayed and wrote '*The Manor House, Hale*'. Turning right into Church Road you retrace your first steps for a short while back to the start.

POINTS OF INTEREST:

St Mary's Church – The ancient church of St Mary's is famed as the last resting place of John Middleton (The Childe of Hale) a 9ft 3in giant who lived in Hale during the late 15th century. His gravestone can be visited on the south side of the church. The church interior has some fine examples of 18th-century architecture.

Hale Lighthouse – Hale lighthouse stands at the tip of Hale Head, the southernmost point of the north Mersey shore. It was from here that Prince Rupert crossed the Mersey with his soldiers. The lighthouse is no longer functional.

REFRESHMENTS:

The Childe of Hale, Hale (tel no: 051 425 2954). Serves a menu of home-made food and traditional local ales.

Walk 33   ALVANLEY AND HELSBY   3½m (6km)

Maps: OS Sheets Landranger 117; Pathfinder SJ 47/57.

A walk with beautiful views.

Start: At 504752, at a fork in the B5393 near Crossley Hospital.

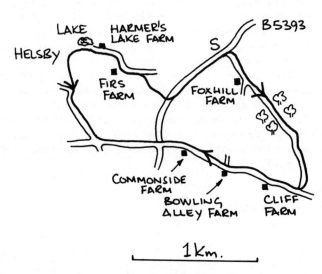

Take the left fork in the road and walk past Fox Hill Farm, and Burrows Lane on your right, to reach Snidley Moore Private Caravan Park on your left. There is a small wood on the right: take the steps that lead into it continuing on a well-defined track that descends left and follows a stream. Cross the stream at a small wooden bridge and bear left to skirt a field. Keeping a small wood to your left continue to a stile. Go over and keep left. Descend wooden steps on your left, go over a stile and follow a track across a field. Go over another stile on to a road. Go right down the road, passing Cliff Farm House on your left to reach **Bowling Alley Farm**.

Continue past dwellings and a small farm on your left to arrive at a crossroads. Go over and continue walking down Back Lane. At a second crossroads go right passing dwellings on both sides of the road. When you reach Hill Side South, a road that branches off to your right, go through a facing gate, then over a low fence on to the

74

National Trust property of Helsby Hill. Follow a path that climbs through trees and after about 100 yards, where the path bears right between outcrops of rock, go forward, crossing a stile on to a rough track. Continue past a pond and Harmers Lake Farm to reach a metalled lane. After Furs farmhouse on your right, the road bears left passing trees. Just before reaching a white cottage to the right, take a footpath on the right that is signed 'Tarvin Road and Commonside'. Go over a stile and cross a field keeping to the left edge. Go over wooden steps and stay to the left to cross another stile. Skirt the left edge of the next field and turn right at a facing fence. Go ahead to reach a stile on your left and go over on to a track that descends to a road. Go left passing Tuehill House on your left on the way back to your car.

POINTS OF INTEREST:

Bowling Alley Farm – It is worth visiting the farm's herb and countryware shop.

In the latter part of the 18th century the mail was carried on horseback from Chester to Warrington via Helsby. A highwayman who robbed the mailman and was eventually caught in Exeter, stood trial at Chester in 1795 and was publicly gibbeted near the scene of his crime on Helsby Hill.

REFRESHMENTS:

Facilities are available in Frodsham.

Walk 34   **MOORE NATURE RESERVE** $3^{1/}_{2}$m (6km)

Maps: OS Sheets Landranger 108; Pathfinder SJ 48/58.

A short walk mostly through an attractive Nature Reserve.

Start: At 578843, the Post Office in Moore.

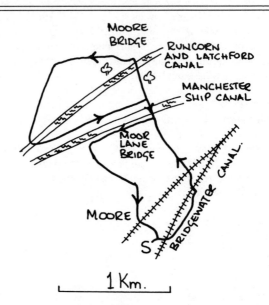

From the Post Office turn right into Runcorn Road. The Red Lion pub is immediately on your right. Follow Runcorn Road for 500 yards going through a staggered roadbridge. The towpath of the Bridgewater Canal (see Walk 9) appears on your right after a further 300 yards, a concrete post pinch gap providing access on to the towpath from the pavement. Turn left and walk for some 700 yards along the canal. Rejoin the main road again where a pinch gap appears in the railings, turning right opposite the village shop. Cross the road, with care, and walk past the Methodist Church. Turn left after 50 yards into Moore Lane and follow it for 400 yards as it gradually descends to the **Moore Lane Swing Bridge**. The bridge provides fine views to the high level Stockton Bridge up river.

    A footpath is provided on the right-hand side of the bridge. Go over to reach, after 50 yards, a narrow crossroads. Walk straight ahead past a sign on your left which

Rosemount

introduces you to Moore Nature Reserve. The next 1 mile of the walk follows a wide circular footpath, which if you keep to the left returns you to the swing bridge.

Turn right into the Promenard Road immediately after crossing the bridge again, and follow the road for $^3/_4$ mile as it gently ascends back to the staggered roadbridge. From there retrace your outward route back to the start.

POINTS OF INTEREST:

Moore Lane Swing Bridge – The swing bridge was one of the last motor-driven bridges to be constructed over the Manchester Ship Canal and remains one of the last still in operation. It was featured, briefly, in the Oscar-winning film '*Yanks* ' which starred Richard Gere.

REFRESHMENTS:

The Red Lion, Runcorn Road, Moore (tel no: 092 574 205).

Walk 35   DUNSDALE   3¹/₂m (6km)

Maps: OS Sheets Landranger 117; Pathfinder SJ 47/57.

A relatively easy walk on good footpaths.

Start: At 523763, a rough parking place in the lane near Beacon Hill.

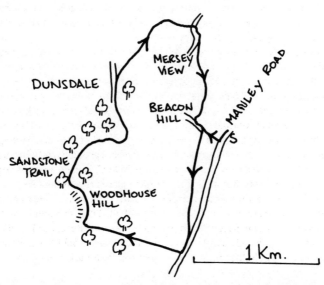

From the parking place, walk towards Manley. Soon you will see small caves on your left, known locally as the **Robbers' Caves**. Turn right into the lane signed for the Forest Hills Hotel. After 200 yards cross a stile on the left where a wooden footpath sign indicates 'Manley Road'. Follow the edge of the field and at its far corner cross a stile and continue along the footpath between the hedge and the wire fence. At a footpath junction, continue along the way signed 'Manley'. From here there are clear views across the Mersey Estuary. After about 600 yards cross a stile on to the farm track and go over the stile on the bank opposite. Follow the path beyond diagonally across a field. You will meet a stile in the hedge on your left about 30 yards from the far left corner of the field.

Go over this on to a road and turn right. Turn right between two cottages where a footpath sign marked 'Woodhouse Hill' indicates the way down a broad track between two hedges. At a crossroads of tracks, continue straight ahead. Your track enters a wood and becomes a path. Soon after this take the right fork and descend through trees to reach the edge of a field. Follow a path through the field keeping the fence on your right. You will encounter Sandstone Trail markers with their distinctive 'S' which will indicate the way on this part of the walk.

Your path bears left, away from the field, after 400 yards and follows an old sandstone wall on the right. Gradually ascend through a wood to reach the crest of a rise. Go over the rise and drop down, steeply at first, then bear right to follow a broad path which runs along the top of **Foxhill Crags.**

After about $^1/_2$ mile the path enters Dunsdale Hollow. Care should be taken when descending the small sandstone outcrop here. Follow the path beneath the cliffs around Dunsdale Hollow, passing a memorial plaque to Jack Baker, a pioneer of Cheshire walks, at a junction of paths. To the right here, a path and staircase lead up to Mersey View, while straight ahead a rocky scramble goes up Jacob's Ladder. Our path goes to the left, continuing around Dunsdale Hollow. Drop gently downhill to reach the end of a road and bear right along a track. The track climbs, then forks by Erindale Cottage. Take the right fork and climb steadily through trees to meet a cobbled road. Go ahead along this to reach a metalled road. Turn right past Hillside Villa, then go up 58 steps on the right to reach the Belle Monte Inn, an excellent place for refreshments.

Leave the Belle Monte through the exit of its car park, on to a road. Turn right and follow the lane uphill towards a large pylon on **Beacon Hill**. After 200 yards leave the lane where a footpath sign on the left indicates Simons Lane and Beacon Hill. Follow the footpath, crossing a stile and then two more stiles after a narrow field. Cross the lane on to the facing track and follow this to reach a lane that leads back to the start.

POINTS OF INTEREST:

Robbers' Caves – Shallow depressions in a sandstone outcrop which provide a pleasant picnic site and a place for children to climb and explore.

Foxhill Crags – A popular venue for local rock climbers. The overhanging cliffs offer very strenuous problems.

Beacon Hill – An excellent viewpoint which is the beginning of the Sandstone Trail which runs across Cheshire to Shropshire.

REFRESHMENTS:

The Forest Hills Hotel, Frodsham (tel no: 0928 35255). An hotel and leisure complex.
The Belle Monte, Frodsham (tel no: 0928 32321).

Walk 36   **DARESBURY**   4m (6.5km)

Maps: OS Sheets Landranger 108; Pathfinder SJ 48/58.

A walk along old country lanes near one of Cheshire's most historic villages.

Start: At 579828, the Sessions House in Daresbury.

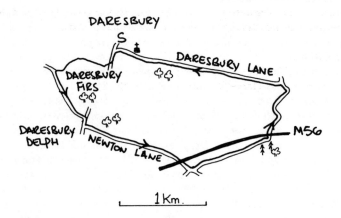

Turn right from the Sessions House and walk up the lane for 500 yards. Go right off the road at a footpath signpost. Follow the sign's direction for 400 yards across arable farmland. Go over a stile before the A56 and proceed, with caution, across the road. Go over another stile on the opposite bank and follow the footpath beyond for 250 yards to the Daresbury Firs plantation. The footpath descends steeply through the plantation to reach a stile. Go over and follow the footpath for 150 yards to Delph Lane. Turn left and walk up the lane for 700 yards to its junction with the A56.

     Once again cross the road with caution and turn right on to the second junction ahead. Walk for 70 yards before turning left into Newton Lane and follow the lane for ³/₄ mile to the next junction. Turn left and walk for 1 mile to the junction of Pillmoss Lane. Turn left, following the road over the M56 motorway. Turn left again after 150 yards into Hatton Lane. Walk around the sharp bends to reach the Hatton Arms and village shop. Turn left at the pub into Daresbury Lane and walk for 1 mile back into the village of Daresbury. **All Saints Parish Church** is the first building to appear on your right as you re-enter the village and 70 yards beyond the church is **the Sessions House** from where you started.

POINTS OF INTEREST:

All Saints Parish Church, Daresbury – A fine old country church which is famed for its stained glass windows and Lewis Carroll memorials. The author of *Alice in Wonderland* was born in the village.

The Sessions House, Daresbury – The Sessions House was built in 1841 and will shortly be converted into the official Lewis Carroll Visitors' Centre.

REFRESHMENTS:

The Ring O' Bells, Chester Road, Daresbury (tel no: 092 574 256).
The Hatton Arms, Warrington Road, Hatton (tel no: 092 573 314).

Walk 37   WILLASTON AND THE WIRRAL WAY   4m (6.5km)

Maps: OS Sheets Landranger 117; Pathfinder SJ 27/37.

An easy walk, fairly level through farmland and along a disused railway converted into a country park.

Start: At 331773, Hadlow Road Station, Willaston.

Adjacent to the car park is the restored **Hadlow Road Station.** At the far end of the platform, a gate leads out on to Hadlow Road. Cross this and go through the gateway opposite. The old railway beyond is now the Wirral Way, a long distance footpath and part of the Wirral Country Park. Follow the Way for about 400 yards. Near an electricity pylon take a footpath down steps to a stile. Go over and turn right here, following the fence to another stile, where you should turn diagonally left across a field. On the opposite side, cross a stile and then keep straight ahead towards Willaston. When you reach the edge of the village, bear left to emerge into the car park of the Pollard Inn where refreshments may be obtained. Go through the car park, but just before the road, take a footpath between the car park and some houses, which leads into the centre of **Willaston** with its attractive village green.

Go past the green and turn left along the B5133. Shortly you will see a church on your right. Turn along a footpath by the side of this. After passing some garages, turn left around the back of the church and then right into a housing estate. Just before the first house, a footpath runs left around the backs of several houses and then out into a sports field. Turn right in the field going along a hedge and over two stiles on to a metalled road. Turn right. On your left you will see **The Old Mill**.

Just beyond the mill take a bridleway on your left beside Mill House. Go down this for 200 yards and then take a footpath on your right signposted for St Hey Lane. Cross a stile and follow a hedge for $^1/_2$ mile – this hedge is the Cheshire county boundary! Cross two more stiles to reach St Hey Lane, a rough bridleway. Turn right and follow the bridleway which, after about 400 yards, becomes a metalled lane that leads to the B5133. Cross into Heath Lane opposite and follow this for about 600 yards. Just before the road climbs to cross the Wirral Way, take a footpath on your right. At the bottom of a slope, turn right, back on to the Wirral Way and follow it back to the car park and start.

POINTS OF INTEREST:

Hadlow Road Station – This has been restored and refurbished to appear just as it would have done on a typical day in 1952, the year the line closed down. Everything has been re-created down to the last detail.

Willaston – Although, it is, today, mostly a modern village, the centre of Willaston is very old, with a number of fascinating buildings, dating from the 16th and 17th centuries, grouped around an attractive village green. Most of these buildings are old farms, the formation now being unique in the Wirral.

The Old Mill – Built in 1800, this was the largest of the old Wirral flour mills. At the top it had five sets of grinding stones, driven by wind and used for grinding cattle food, while on the ground floor there were four sets of bigger grinding stones, driven by steam, for making wheat into flour. In 1930 a storm broke its sails and it was forced to close. Today it is a rather unusual private house.

REFRESHMENTS:

The Pollard Inn, Willaston (tel no: 051 327 4615).

Walk 38   THE MANCHESTER SHIP CANAL   4m (6½km)

Maps: OS Sheets Landranger 109; Pathfinder SJ 68/78.

An easy fairly level walk through farmland and along canal paths.

Start: At 652875, the car park behind the Pickering Arms.

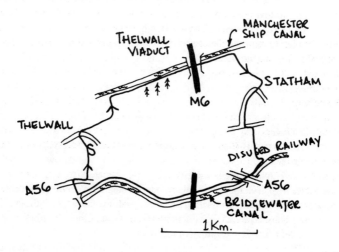

Turn left out of the car park and take a footpath immediately on the right past the village Post Office. Go past the rear of several houses. The marshy area on your left here was once the course of the River Mersey, before the Manchester Ship Canal was constructed. The path reaches a stile. Do not go over this, but turn left down some steps. Cross two footbridges and a stile to reach the **Manchester Ship Canal**. Turn right up a bank above the canal.

After 50 yards, drop down again and follow the footpath/bridleway along the canal for 1 mile. This will take you under the infamous Thelwall Viaduct which carries the M6 over the canal. Just beyond the first stile after the viaduct, turn right along a footpath, away from the canal. The path soon becomes a wide track: follow it to its junction with another. Turn right to reach a metalled road at a sharp bend. Go right and at a T-junction turn left. After 50 yards take a footpath on your right over a stile and follow a path through a small wooded area and over a disused railway. On the other side of the railway go around the front of cottages to reach the towpath of the Bridgewater Canal (see Walk 9).

Keep beside the canal for $1^1/_2$ miles, passing beneath the M6 again. Just before reaching the first bridge over the canal after the motorway turn right away from the canal into a small car park. Go out on to a rough track, which crosses the disused railway again and goes down to the A56. Turn right and after 100 yards take a footpath on the left, which leads through a new housing estate, emerging into a park. Go straight ahead here, passing to the right of swings to reach a rough road on to the main road through Thelwall. Turn left to return to the car park, on the way passing the **Pickering Arms** where refreshments may be obtained.

POINTS OF INTEREST:

Manchester Ship Canal – This was built between 1887 and 1894 to allow ocean-going vessels to reach Manchester and so avoid heavy dock dues at Liverpool. It was financed by cotton mill owners and its opening made Manchester the industrial capital of Britain. The canal, which is 36 miles long and over 30ft deep, required 82 million tons of earth to be excavated.

Pickering Arms – On the wall of this pub is an inscription which reads: '*In the year 923, King Edward the Elder founded a Cyty here and called it Thelwall*'. This relates to a series of forts along the Mersey (of which Thelwall was one) which Edward built to keep out the Danes, who had conquered Northern England.

REFRESHMENTS:
The Pickering Arms, Thelwall (tel no: 0925 61001).

Walk 39   **HESWALL VILLAGE TO PARKGATE**   4m (6.5km)

Maps: OS Sheets Landranger 108 and 117; Pathfinder SJ 28/38 and SJ 27/37.

A fine circular walk.

Start: The car park in Pye Road beside the Heswall Bus Station.

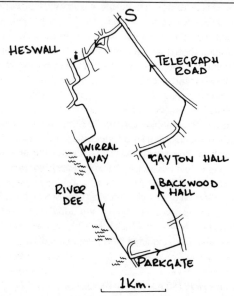

From the bus station, cross Telegraph Road (the A540) and turn left. A walk of about 100 yards will bring you to Rocky Lane. Turn right into it and follow it as it drops down to the War Memorial. Turn right into Deeview Road and, almost immediately, left into School Hill continuing downhill to the old village. With the Black Horse Hotel on your right, cross the road to Heswall Church, beautifully sited overlooking the Dee, and enter the footpath which leads down through the churchyard to Rectory Lane. Turn left on entering this lane and right, into Station Road, on leaving it. A short walk will bring you to Riverbank Road and here your way is left. As the road bears right look for the sign directing you to the Wirral Way. Turn right along the Way passing under a bridge and over a cart-track, to reach the entrance to Heswall Golf Links. Continue forward to the next gate on the right, a wooden bachelor gate admitting you to the golf course.

86

Walk straight across towards the Dee and, on reaching the sea-wall, go left along it to reach **Parkgate** sea-front, a good place to stop for refreshments with its quaint cafés, pubs and Parkgate home-made ice-cream, famous throughout the area.

Leave The Square and walk along School Lane, passing the Old Schoolhouse and shortly reaching Brookland Road. Continue ahead, passing a modern school and, after walking under a wooden footbridge, take a footpath that leads you to the open country again. Where the path ends at Wood Lane go left along this quiet lane to reach busy Boathouse Lane. Go straight across on to a broad path, signed 'Public Footpath to Gayton'. This path leads you between Backwood Farm and Backwood Hall. Where it bears to the right, go straight ahead through a bachelor gate and into a field. Drop down to go over a stile, a footbridge and further stile. After crossing the stream, continue straight ahead across the next field and then look ahead for a three-bar step-stile which allows you to reach a footpath alongside the golf course. Go forward with the hedge on your right. Soon the path leaves the golf course and leads into a broad, but muddy, track which ends at the cobblestones of Gayton village, close to **Gayton Hall**.

At the crossroads beyond Gayton Hall turn right and proceed up Well Lane, a quiet avenue which, after a walk of about 10 minutes, will bring you to Dawstone Road. Turn left and, after walking a few yards, cross the road to reach a footpath running between houses. Turn left at the far end of this path for a short walk along Telegraph Road back to the car park.

POINTS OF INTEREST:

Parkgate – The village can boast an historic past. Philip Sulley, writing in 1889, said: *'Parkgate in the last century was thronged with passengers to and from Ireland, from Bagilt and Flint, to which places ferry packets sailed daily, and with visitors from all parts of the country to the year 1820, when the rapid silting up of the river prevented vessels of any size from approaching the New Quay, and gradually the place waned and dropped away, and is now only a summer resort'.*

Gayton Hall – Was the home of the famous Glegg family which settled in Wirral in 1380. Like so many old houses it has been altered and added to throughout the centuries. During the time that Parkgate was the chief port of embarkation for Ireland, it was famed for the hospitality shown to travellers. In 1689, King William III stayed the night here and, on leaving the next day, knighted his host, William Glegg.

REFRESHMENTS:
Several in Parkgate.

Walk 40   CULCHETH AND CROFT   4¹/₂m (7.5km)

Maps: OS Sheets Landranger 109; Pathfinder SJ 69/79.

An easy, fairly level walk through farmland and along a disused railway.

Start: At 649949, the car park at Culcheth Linear Park.

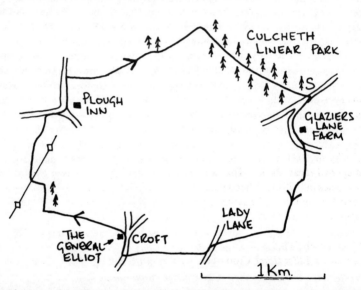

From the car park, walk towards the railway bridge. Do not go under it, but turn right up steps to Wigshaw Lane. Turn right along this and after 100 yards go left into Glaziers Lane. Just beyond Glaziers Lane Farm, take a footpath on the right through a gap in the hedge and follow the hedge on your left. After 400 yards an obsolete stile and a signpost are reached. Turn right across the field to another stile (signposted for Lady Lane) and keep straight ahead across several fields to reach Lady Lane. Turn left into the lane and after 50 yards take a footpath on your right. Cross the field to a stile and then keep straight ahead to a large tree in the middle of the next field. Here bear slightly left to reach a gap in the hedge opposite. A path beyond leads between high hedges and emerges by the garage in Croft. Turn right along the road, and soon you will reach a road junction, beside which is The General Elliot where refreshments may be obtained.

Take the left fork past the pub and, after 100 yards, take a footpath on the left. Beyond Mount Pleasant House this disappears so keep straight ahead towards a solitary tree. Just beyond this turn right along an old field boundary, marked by a line of solitary oaks. After the last three, you will reach a cladded wooden post. Turn left here past an electricity pylon and then right, walking parallel to the overhead cables. At another solitary oak tree turn left on to a track coming from a farm and almost immediately right, heading in the direction of an electricity pylon, to reach Stone Pit Lane. Turn right along this into the hamlet of New Lane End. Turn left at a T-junction and, after 200 yards, take a footpath on your right. This runs beside a ditch at first, but then crosses the ditch into an open field. After a short distance beside a hedge, head diagonally left across a field, to a solitary clump of trees, where you will meet a rough track. Follow this around the trees to a path junction. Go directly across this passing under a telegraph line. After passing through a gap in a hedge, walk straight across the field to a pinch gap opposite. There a flight of steps drops down into Culcheth Linear Park. Turn right now along the bed of an old railway track. This is pleasantly wooded and is an attractive end to the walk as you cover the last mile back to the car park.

POINTS OF INTEREST:

Culcheth Linear Park – This was originally the Wigan to Glazebrook railway, constructed in 1878 to aid the commercial extraction of peat from Risley Moss. The line closed down in 1965 and was then converted into the lovely country park which exists today.

REFRESHMENTS:

The General Elliot Hotel, Croft (tel no: 092 576 3264).

Walk 41   HATCHMERE AND KINGSLEY   4³/₄m (8km)

Maps: OS Sheets Landranger 117; Pathfinder SJ 47/57.
A walk along some of the old green roads of Cheshire.
Start: At 554722, the car park at the Hatchmere Picnic Area.

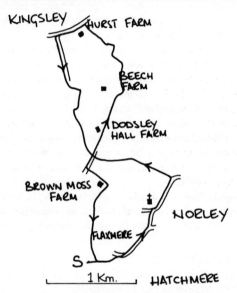

Turn right out of the car park and follow the track alongside the picnic area. Where the track bears left after 150 yards, go straight ahead taking the right branch at a fork after 10 yards. Join a metalled road, beside a cottage built in 1833, and follow it to the junction of lanes. Turn left up School Lane and walk up this, past a primary school, built as a Sunday School in 1838. Continue to a junction near Norley Parish Church. Turn right, then left up a lane signposted for Crowton. Where the lane bears right by a cottage built in 1697 go left on to a track between the cottage and The Oranges and continue ahead on a track indicated by the Public Footpath sign. Go between two hedgerows then along the left edge of a field. Cross a stile at the far corner, go over a track and drop down the slope to the wet hollow below. Cross the stream by a footbridge and go uphill. Go over a stile and climb the small hillside ahead. Bear left to the edge of a field and follow this past an unsightly tip. Turn left at a fence and follow it towards new farm buildings.

Before these are reached, turn right and walk across the field to a hedge on the far side. A stile by a gate on the right gives access to a lane. Turn right, go past Beech Farm, and on for $^1/_2$ mile to reach a gate to the left by a double bend sign. Go through the gate, signposted for Kingsley, down a short track, then left across an old stone stile. Go right across the field and cross a stile at the corner of holly bushes. Follow the fence to the right, then turn left at the corner and walk up for 40 yards to reach a gap concealing a stile. Cross this then turn left and follow the hedge to reach a stile in the corner. Cross this and turn right along a track.

The track leads to the village of Kingsley. Turn left and walk past Hurst Methodist Church and Hurst Farm to join a larger road. Turn left on to the track signposted as a bridleway. Follow this between two high banks at first, then between fields, flanked by hedges and fences. The bridleway becomes a path which runs between facing field boundaries to meet a track past Dodsley Hall Farm. Follow the track past Dodsley Farm to meet a lane, opposite the stile you crossed earlier on your way from Hatchmere. Go right to a crossroads. Turn left and walk to Brownmoss Farm on the right. Enter the yard, just past the buildings, and follow the way indicated by the bridleway sign past outbuildings to a stile. Go over and follow a broad track over two stiles and on to a small gate before a lane and a cottage.

Go right on the lane and, shortly, join another lane. Continue ahead to where you will see **Flaxmere** on your left. Soon after this the lane reaches the picnic area near **Hatchmere**.

POINTS OF INTEREST:

Flaxmere – Once an open stretch of water like Hatchmere, it has been filled with sediment but is still unsuitable land for farming.

Hatchmere – A lovely Cheshire mere, believed to have been created by a huge block of ice left behind at the end of the last Ice Age.

REFRESHMENTS:

Forest Café, Hatchmere (tel no: 0928 88557).

The Carriers Inn, near the car park (tel no: 0928 88258).

Walk 42 BURTONWOOD AND THE SANKEY VALLEY 5m (8km)
Maps: OS Sheets Landranger 108; Pathfinder SJ 49/59.
An easy walk, fairly level across fields and along a canal towpath.
Start: At 565929, the car park next to the Chapel House Inn, Burtonwood.

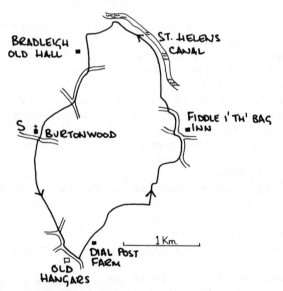

From the car park turn left past the pub and church. On the right you will see a social club and beside this a footpath leading between houses. Follow this to open countryside. Keep ahead beside a hedge and then a fence to where the footpath meets a broad track. Turn left and then immediately right, crossing a large field to a broken stile beside some solitary trees. On its far side drop down on to a metalled road, through a pinch gap. Turn right to reach the Warrington-Burtonwood road. Go left. Ahead you will now see some large buildings. These are old hangars, lone survivors of the now vanished **Burtonwood Airfield**.

After 400 yards take a footpath on the left along a farm access road. Pass through the farmyard on its left and go round a large pond. Follow the hedge for $^1/_2$ mile into a wild and overgrown area. Keep to the left through this, swinging around to the right alongside a fence. After 400 yards turn left along a signposted footpath. The path crosses a large field divided by Phipps Brook, over which there is a footbridge. On the other side turn right on to a broad track and follow this to a metalled road. Turn left along this, to its junction with Alder Lane. Opposite is the Fiddle i' th' Bag Inn where refreshments are available. Turn left and then immediately right. After 400 yards take a footpath right, go over a footbridge crossing Sankey Brook and then diagonally left across a field on a well-defined route to reach the towpath of a restored section of the **St Helens Canal**.

Bear left along the towpath and follow it for over 1 mile through the attractive parkland of the Sankey Valley Linear Park. When you reach the second bridge over the canal, turn left across a footbridge back over Sankey Brook and then bear right uphill. At the top of a short climb turn left along a broad footpath. Soon you will pass the access road leading to **Bradlegh Old Hall**.

Carry straight on past the access road to reach a metalled road. Turn right along this to a T-junction, on the edge of Burtonwood. Opposite is a footpath skirting the edge of a housing estate. Take this and follow it to emerge on to the main village road near to the church. Turn right to return to the car park.

POINTS OF INTEREST:

Burtonwood Airfield – Formerly an RAF base, it was taken over, in 1942, by the Americans who used it as a maintenance and repair unit. A huge warehouse built in 1956 is still the largest covered storage depot in Europe.

St Helens Canal – Opened in 1757, this was the first stillwater navigation in England. It was constructed to carry coal from St Helens to Liverpool and stimulated the growth of the chemical industry in Widnes.

Bradlegh Old Hall – Surrounding the 19th-century farmhouse are the remains of Sir Peter Legh's fortified manor house built in 1465. Surviving today are the gatehouse, with its tiny chapel and the moat. In the farmhouse is an old bed in which Richard III is reputed to have slept.

REFRESHMENTS:

The Chapel House Inn, Burtonwood (tel no: 092 52 5607).
The Fiddle i' th' Bag, Burtonwood (tel no: 092 52 5442).

Walk 43   THE RIVER WEAVER   5m (8km)

Maps: OS Sheets Landranger 117; Pathfinder SJ 47/57.

A lovely peaceful walk along the river bank and over farmland.

Start: At 561782, just outside the village of Aston.

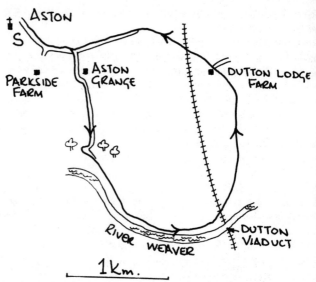

Walk down the lane passing a signed driveway 'Private Road to Parkside Farm Only'. Follow the lane to the right passing a facing private road and continue past a large farm on the left. Go on to farm outbuildings, pass these and then go right at facing trees, descending to arrive at the end of a lane and reach a gate. Go through and cross the field bearing diagonally right to reach the towpath of the **River Weaver**.

Facing the river, go left, keeping to the towpath over two stiles, and passing dwellings on the left. Go through a gate and continue to arrive shortly at a large footbridge which crosses an inlet of the river. Do not cross the bridge but go left, then forward along the left bank of the inlet to arrive at a stile. Go over and keeping to the right of facing trees go on to a stile in a crossing fence. Go over and along a grassy track which leads on to a lane. Go left climbing towards Dutton Lodge Farm. Continue through the farmyard, going between outbuildings and taking the next turn left.

Descend on to a well-defined track and take it, going through a gate and climbing slightly to pass through a tunnel under the railway. Follow the track ahead which bears right through a field. Keep ahead through two fields to reach a lane. Go right now to follow the lane back to your car.

POINTS OF INTEREST:

River Weaver – The Weaver is the only large river to rise and flow its full course within Cheshire.

Rock salt was discovered near Winsford in 1670 and the river was primarily made navigable to transport it. Although the salt is still mined in this area pleasure craft now account for the majority of traffic.

Walk 44　　**ACTON BRIDGE AND CUDDINGTON**　　5m (8km)

Maps: OS Sheets Landranger 117 and 118; Pathfinder SJ 47/57 and SJ 67/77.

Across fields and along lanes in a quiet part of north Cheshire.
Start: At 599747, the car park of Acton Bridge railway station.

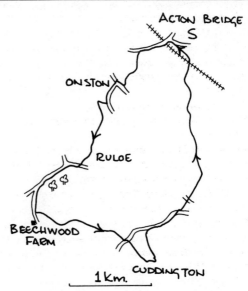

Turn left out of the car park, then cross the railway bridge. Follow the road out of the village and turn left just after Milton Baptist Church into a lane marked 'No Through Road'. After 50 yards the lane bends and forks. Take the right fork, go over a footbridge and walk past 'Glan y Dwr' and 'Brookside' to a stile on the left. Cross this and go across a field to another stile. Go over and turn right along a track, then left along a lane. Walk through Onston, beyond which your lane bears left. Leave it at this point and go through a gate next to an old stile on the left. Follow the hedge on your right, then bear left at the next corner and continue following the right-hand hedge to a stile in the far corner. Cross and walk over the field to the gateway in the facing hedge. Continue to the facing stile, go over and on to another stile in the far right corner. Go over this stile, and follow the small brook, subsequently crossing two more stiles to reach a lane.

Turn right and walk past Bent Lane in the direction of Norley. Go past Ruloe Cottage and walk uphill to the hamlet of Ruloe. Turn left at the junction. Go downhill for 400 yards then, just before the entrance to Beechwood Farm, cross a stile to the left under a footpath sign. Cross a field, go over an earth-topped bridge and walk uphill, with a fence and the Home Farm on your right. Cross a stile by a gate and walk on beside a fence over the top of the hill and down the other side. Cross a stile on the right and drop steeply down between blackberry bushes and a wooden fence. Where there is a choice of stiles, take the one on the left and walk uphill with trees on your right. Cross two more stiles then follow a track to its junction with a lane.

Turn left, then right up a track. At a facing gate turn right and follow a footpath to a bridge above a small waterfall. Continue beside the mere, then bear left at a path junction and walk to a crossing lane. Turn left and follow the lane past a small group of houses and then uphill to the junction by Cuddington Methodist Church. Turn right and follow a lane down and over a stream. About 70 yards after Mill House turn left on to a footpath reached through a kissing gate. Walk under the trees and go through a gap in a wire fence. Go up to a track and follow it to a crossing lane.

Go over the stile almost opposite and walk straight across a field to a facing stile and footbridge. Cross and go over the next field towards a house. Cross two stiles to reach a gate before the house drive. Turn left and follow the fence on your right. Go over the bar stile in the short crossing hedge and follow the fence on your left, crossing four stiles. After the fourth stile, leave the ditch by way of an earth bridge and bear diagonally right to a footbridge in the facing hedge. Cross and go uphill with trees on your left. At the top of the hill keep beside the fence to reach a stile. Cross and turn to cross a second stile on the right. Follow the fence on your left down the field and cross a stile on to the railway line. Go over the footbridge, then follow the path to a lane. Turn left here and walk back to the railway station and your car.

REFRESHMENTS:

The Hazel Pear Inn, Acton Bridge (tel no: 0606 853195). This comfortable pub offers a good menu for bar snacks together with two or three daily specials on a blackboard. There is an adventure playground for children, and a bowling green.

Walk 45 **WHITEGATE AND THE RIVER WEAVER** $5^1/_4$m (8.5km)
Maps: OS Sheets Landranger 118; Pathfinder SJ 67/77 and
SJ 66/76.
An easy walk across farmland and along the River Weaver.
Start: At 646713, the car park below Hartford Bridge.

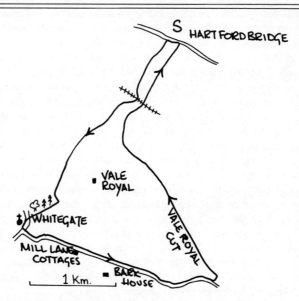

Walk back up the steep track used to reach the car park and turn left along the lane which
is signposted 'Public Footpath' as it leaves the A556. Follow the tree-lined lane under
a railway viaduct and past a car park. Continue to a second car park, where you will see
stone steps leading up through rhododendron bushes on your right. Go up the steps and
on to a stile before an enormous field. Go over and take the well-trodden path across
the field to the wood on the far side. Follow the path through the wood to reach another
very large field. Walk through the crops which are grown without boundaries. On your
left you will see a large house. This is **Vale Royal**.

When you reach a wood, turn left and walk along the edge of the field for 100
yards. Step over a stile and join the drive to Vale Royal. Turn right and follow the drive
beneath huge beech trees. Leave the park opposite St Mary's Church. Turn left into the

village of Whitegate. Turn left by the thatched Whitegate Cottage and walk up Grange Lane. Bear left into Mill Lane. Follow Mill Lane for approximately 1 mile, passing Bark House Farm on your right. The lane, which has been straight, bears right then left and drops downhill past Mill House, a restored water mill. Cross a bridge over the stream, then leave the lane for the track on the left. Walk over the two bridges across the River Weaver (see Walk 43). Turn left and follow the riverside path for almost 2 miles, passing **Vale Royal Locks**. When you reach Hartford Bridge you will find a path on the right which climbs up to join the A556. Walk across the bridge to rejoin your car.

POINTS OF INTEREST:

Vale Royal – Formerly the largest Cistercian Abbey in England. Built by Edward I. The remains of this once great church have disappeared. The large house now standing on the site was built for the Cholmondley family.

Vale Royal Locks – These were constructed during the canalisation of the river. During 1860-70 the locks were doubled to give a basin of 100ft by 22ft. They were later extended to a width of 42ft.

REFRESHMENTS:

The Blue Cap, Sandiway (tel no: 0606 883006). Named after a former hound of the Cheshire Hunt, this pub is located beside the A556, approximately 2 miles from Hartford Bridge. It serves bar snacks and has an à la carte restaurant which is open in the evening.

Walks 46 and 47 **MOULDSWORTH AND MANLEY** 5¹/₄m (8.5km)
Maps: OS Sheets Landranger 117; Pathfinder SJ 47/57 & 46/56.
An easy walk through pastoral Cheshire.
Start: At 511704, on the B5393 at the bottom of the hill below The
Goshawk.

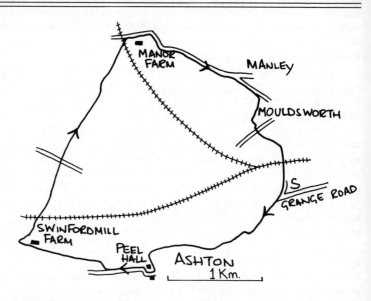

Go along the lane towards Ashton to where Grange Road joins it and cross the stile on
the right there, signed 'Great Barrow 5¹/₂km, Chester 12km'. Follow the hedge on your
left for 150 yards, then go through the gate to the left and walk along the hedge, crossing
three stiles. Go over a lane and walk down the drive ahead to Peel Hall. Go into the
farmyard, then turn right after the large barn and walk along it to a gate. Go through,
then through the adjoining gate on your right and follow a track, bearing left after 60
yards. Go along the straight track to a gate. Go through and past a pond to reach the end
of a field. Go through a gate on your right and walk with a hedge on your left. After 100
yards bear right across the field to a stile at the right corner of a crossing hedge. Go over
and walk with a fence on your right. Cross the stile by a gate, next to Swinford Mill
Cottage, turn left and walk to the entrance of Training Farm, on your right.

Turn into the entrance and go past the Dutch barn. Cross a stile, then walk along the concrete shelf between a building and the stream. A gate at the rear of the building allows you into a field. Go across to a gate in the far fence. Go through to the railway embankment. Using stiles – and taking care! – cross the railway line. Walk across a field to a gate in the diagonally opposite corner. Go through and walk down the narrow field. Go through the facing gate and continue past a pond to a lane. Go over the stile opposite, signed 'Manley' and walk with the fence on your right. Cross a stile and footbridge, then bear left of a pond which is encircled by trees. Join the hedge on your left and go through the gate in it. Continue with the hedge on your right, cross a footbridge and walk to the railway bridge where a gate allows access to a lane.

Turn right and walk under the bridge, then bear right past Manor Farm. Follow the road up through a rock cutting, past Manley Post Office – where there is a view to Tarvin Church, with its square tower, about 3 miles away – and on to Mouldsworth Methodist Church.

Just before the church, climb an old stile on the right. Follow a line of trees, then turn left at the facing hedge. After 20 yards go through a gap in the hedge and walk across the next field, bearing left to arrive at a gate behind the houses. Go through and walk down the track to a lane. Turn right to reach the Police Station. If you were to continue along this road you would reach **Mouldsworth Motor Museum** after about $^1/_2$ mile. The walk turns left after the Police Station and continues down the drive to Rose Bank Farm. Go ahead at the point where the drive bears right and follow the fence to a crossing lane. Turn right and walk past The Goshawk to your car.

POINTS OF INTEREST:

Mouldsworth Motor Museum – Over 50 vintage to classic cars and motorcycles are on display. The museum is open every Sunday, 12.00–5.00pm in summer and 12.00–dusk in winter. To reach it by car, drive uphill past The Goshawk then turn left after $^1/_4$ mile into Smithy Lane. The museum will be seen on the left after $^3/_4$ mile.

REFRESHMENTS:
The Goshawk, Mouldsworth (tel no: 09284 302).

Walk 48   **WALTON AND HILL CLIFFE**   5¹/₂m (9km)

Maps: OS Sheets Landranger 108 and 109; Pathfinder SJ 48/58 and SJ 68/78.

An easy walk, with one short climb.

Start: At 600852, the car park at Walton Hall.

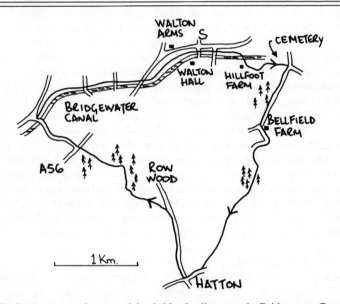

Opposite the entrance to the car park is a bridge leading over the Bridgewater Canal to **Walton Hall**. Beside the bridge, on the left, are some steps: take these down to the canal towpath. Turn left and walk to the next bridge. Leave the towpath here and cross the bridge. On the far side, take a footpath on the left, initially beside the canal, but soon turning right away from it over a stile, towards Hillfoot Farm. Go over another stile, around the farm and turn left uphill beside a fence. At the top of the field bear left to a stile. Go over this and then another on the right into a narrow, hedged pathway. The path emerges into a wide field with many gorse bushes. Continue past a cemetery to reach the top of **Hill Cliffe**.

At the crossroads ahead, turn right into Firs Lane and walk through a residential area. After 400 yards the road enters a deep rocky cut. About half-way along this is the

Wishing Well. Walk out of the cut and at a junction turn left past Bellfield Farm ('Private Drive' sign here applies to cars not pedestrians). The track veers around to the right, goes through a gate and past a large house. Beyond the house leave the track where it bears right and carry straight on along a grassy lane. Cross a stream and climb out of the woodland to emerge into open fields. Follow a broad track with a hedge on your left. Go through a gap in the hedge to where the footpath narrows and passes a wood with ponds in it. From here a well-defined path crosses several fields to reach a gate, which gives access to a rough road. Go straight on into the centre of Hatton.

A left turn at the junction with the B5356 leads to the Hatton Arms, but the route goes right (towards Warrington). After $^1/_2$ mile leave the road over a stile to the left. Go straight on, then turn right over another stile. Bear diagonally left across a field, go through a wide gap and then walk beside a ditch, to reach a stile into Rows Wood. Go over and through the wood crossing a footbridge over a tiny stream. Climb the hillside opposite and turn right along the edge of the wood which eventually bears left. Near a footbridge leave the wood and go ahead across a field, then bear left to a signpost on the edge of more woodland. Turn right here down to the A56. Cross this into Hobb Lane and follow this into the village of Moore. Go over a canal bridge and then left on to the canal towpath. Turn left along the towpath to go back under the bridge. Follow the path for $1^1/_2$ miles through Higher Walton and past the Walton Arms to return to the steps back up to the car park.

POINTS OF INTEREST:

Walton Hall – The hall is an Elizabethan revival house, built in 1836. It was the former home of the Greenhall family, founders of the Greenhall Whitley Brewery in Warrington. The hall and gardens were given to the people of Warrington in 1941. The gardens are now a Country Park.

Hill Cliffe – A good viewpoint over Warrington and the surrounding area. To the west is the Runcorn-Widnes Bridge and Fiddlers Ferry Power Station. To the north the slender spire of Warrington parish church can be seen with, in the background, Winter Hill and its TV transmitter.

The Wishing Well – An old horse trough, cut into the rock of a deep cutting, which was the Old Chester Road. It is fed by a natural spring and during the last century became known as a wishing well. People still drop money in it to make a wish.

REFRESHMENTS:

The Hatton Arms, Hatton (tel no: 092 573 314).
The Walton Arms, Higher Walton (tel no: 0925 62659).

Walk 49 GRAPPENHALL AND THE LUMB BROOK VALLEY 5¹/₂m (9km)

Maps: OS Sheets Landranger 109; Pathfinder SJ 68/78.

A fairly level walk across fields, along a canal towpath and up a wooded valley.

Start: At 637838, the lay-by on the B5356, just south of Appleton.

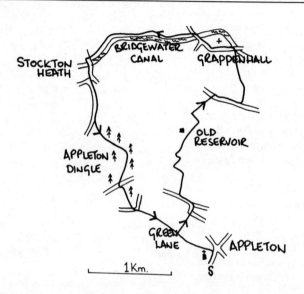

From the car park walk into the centre of the village. At the road junction next to the church, you will see **Appleton Thorn**. Beside the church is Green Lane: turn into this and follow it for about ¹/₂ mile. Beyond an old cottage, take the signposted footpath to the right, going over a stile and following a hedge to reach a metalled road. Turn left along this to a T-junction. Go left again, and after 200 yards take a footpath on the right, following a hedge to a stile beside a signpost. Go over the stile and bear left following the field boundary around to the right to another stile. Go over this and on to a signpost. Turn right there, across the field. On the other side, beyond a stile, bear left uphill to an old reservoir, surrounded by a ruined brick wall. Pass to the right of this and bear left to reach a hedge. The footpath follows this, then goes through a gap on to a wide track. Follow this track to a metalled road. Turn right and after 400 yards take a footpath through a gate on the left. The path heads towards Grappenhall. As you approach the school, the footpath goes through a narrow entry. At the end of this you will reach a rough road beside the Bridgewater Canal. Turn left along this and then left again on to a cobbled street through Grappenhall village. To your right is ancient **Grappenhall Church**.

At the end of the village street, turn right to return to the canal. Cross a bridge, drop down to the towpath and turn right towards Stockton Heath. After about 1 mile the canal crosses Limb Brook Road. Just before this, drop down right and go left under the bridge. After about 100 yards turn right and then immediately left into Dale Lane. The stream on your left is Lumb Brook. When the road begins to turn away from this, leave it and go straight on along a pavement which fronts some houses. This soon gives way to a footpath which is the start of the Lumb Brook Valley Park, known locally as Appleton Dingle. Keep to this footpath along the brook which winds through an attractive wooded valley. After about 1 mile you will reach a metalled road that crosses the valley. Turn left, cross the bridge and continue upstream on the opposite bank. This next section is known as Fords Rough. After $^1/_2$ mile you reach another metalled road. Opposite is a footpath, the end of Green Lane, which you used at the beginning of the walk. Follow this back into Appleton to return to your car.

POINTS OF INTEREST:

Appleton Thorn – A cutting from the Glastonbury Thorn which is said to have sprung from Joseph of Arimathea's staff. On June 29th, children dance around the thorn in a ceremony known as Barning the Thorn. This has its origins in a pagan fertility rite.

Grappenhall Church – A beautiful church, dating mostly from the 16th century, notable for its ancient Saxon font and 14th-century stained glass windows in the south wall. On the church tower is the figure of a cat with a grin, which may be the original Cheshire cat.

REFRESHMENTS:

The Thorn Inn, Appleton (tel no: 0925 64362).
The Ramshead Hotel, Grappenhall (tel no: 0925 62814).

Walk 50 BARNBRIDGE GATES AND PRIMROSE HILL $5^1/_2$m (9km)
Maps: OS Sheets Landranger 118; Pathfinder SJ 47/57 & 46/56.
The first part of this walk follows the Sandstone Trail.
Start: At 542716, the Barnbridge Gates car park.

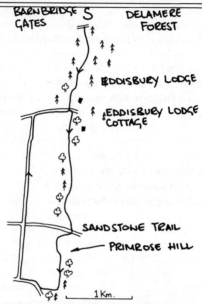

Climb the steps by the side of the car park and turn left along the track into the forest. A sign indicates 'Forest Visitors Centre, 2km'. After 400 yards fork right by a picnic table. Go ahead at the crossroads a little further on to reach a bridge over the railway line. Walk on to a stile on the right. Go over on to a path which follows a bank and a fence to another stile. Cross and turn left, then right on to a track which is signposted for Beeston Castle. Go past Eddisbury Lodge Cottage and continue under **Eddisbury Hill** to reach a road.

Cross the road (beware of fast traffic!) and turn left into a car park. Go down a long flight of wooden steps and bear right at the bottom. Follow a path along a fence and then go uphill, at first through a wood and then under a distinctive line of Scots pines. Go over a stile and walk with a field on your left for a few yards until the path bears right uphill into the forest. The path levels out on Primrose Hill and then reaches a fork.

Leave the Sandstone Trail here, ignoring the track which drops down to the left and taking the path ahead. The path descends through trees to reach a forest road. Turn right and walk out on to a lane.

Turn right and follow the lane downhill to Th'ouse at Top pub. Cross the main road and continue up Yeld Lane ahead. After 1 mile the lane turns sharp left by Howarth's Fruit Farm. Go right here, up a track signposted to 'Sandstone Trail'. Go between gateposts and continue to Eddisbury Lodge. Cross the stile on the left and make your way back along the earlier route to **Barnbridge Gates** and your car.

POINTS OF INTEREST:

Eddisbury Hill – The site of an Iron Age hill fort.

Barnbridge Gates – Formerly a sandstone quarry. At this place, on a quiet morning, wild birds will accept nuts offered from your hand, if you are prepared to be still and patient.

REFRESHMENTS:

Th'ouse at Top (tel no: 0829 517484).
The Forest Café, Hatchmere (tel no: 0928 88557).
The Carrier Inn, Hatchmere (tel no: 0928 88258).

Walk 51   **GREAT BARROW**   5½m (9km)

Maps: OS Sheets Landranger 117; Pathfinder SJ 46/56.

A gently undulating walk through farmland and along the course of a Roman Road.

Start: At 469684, the church in Great Barrow.

From the car park, pass a telephone box and turn left into Ferma Lane. At a junction keep straight ahead. Beyond Greysfield House the lane becomes a rough track and bends right, gently descending with views left across the Gowy Valley. After 400 yards the footpath bears left, then right. At a junction of footpaths keep straight ahead going uphill. Where the footpath bears right and left, cross a stile on the right and continue climbing beside a hedge. Follow the hedge around to the left and go down some stone steps in the field corner, to a farm road. Turn right along this to reach the B5132. Opposite is the Foxcote Inn, where refreshments may be obtained.

    Go left and then right into Broomhill Lane. Follow this to the hamlet of Broomhill. Turn left at the next road junction. After 100 yards take a footpath on the right up a farm road. Go through the farmyard, turn right beyond a gate and go over a stile. Keep ahead and cross a series of stiles, each marked with yellow arrows. After the fifth, veer slightly left to cross a stile and footbridge, and reach a narrow entry which passes terraced cottages to emerge into Irons Lane. Turn left to a junction with Barrow Lane. Turn right past The Old Farm and where the road veers sharply to the right, take the farm road footpath on the left. Follow this towards Park Hall, but just before reaching it, take a footpath on your right over a stile. (Do not go through farmyard, as shown on the map; the footpath has been diverted).

Turn left along a hedge and at a gate, cross a stile and turn right along the other side of the hedge to reach a step-stile. Cross this and go left. After 50 yards turn left through a gate and then right along the opposite side of the hedge. After 400 yards you reach another step-stile which crosses a ditch. Turn right to reach a stile in the corner of a field. You are now following the course of a **Roman Road**.

Go over the stile and go straight on beside the hedge, crossing three more stiles to reach a metalled road at the edge of Stamford Bridge. Go right to a T-junction in the centre of the village. Turn right along the B5132 and after the last house, take a footpath on the right through a kissing gate and bear slightly right along the hedge. Go past a cottage to a stile and footbridge. Cross these and head diagonally right across an open field in the direction of Great Barrow Church perched on the hillside beyond. At the far side of the field a bridge leads over a brook to a stile. Beyond a wide track climbs up to the B5132. Turn right along this into **Great Barrow**. Just short of the village, take a narrow lane right up to Great Barrow Church. To return to the car park, follow the lane around to the left back to the B5132.

POINTS OF INTEREST:

The Roman Road – This was Watling Street North which joined Chester to Manchester. Sections of the raised mound or *agger* on which the road was constructed can still be seen in the hedge.

Great Barrow Church – This beautifully situated church is dedicated to St Bartholomew and dates from 1744. It has an interesting and unusual 'bulls-eye' window and inside there is a register of rectors going back to 1313.

REFRESHMENTS:

The Foxcote Inn, Little Barrow (tel no: 0244 301145).

Walk 52   LITTLE BUDWORTH   2³/₄m (4km)

Maps: OS Sheets Landranger 117; Pathfinder SJ 46/56.

A very easy walk on good paths with no climbing.

Start: The car park at Little Budworth Country Park.

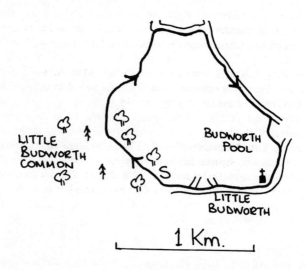

Go over the road from the car park and take a short track to a sandy cross-track. Turn right and go ahead for about 450 yards to a junction of tracks. Turn right. Cross the road and continue along the track opposite, ignoring the private drive leading off right. Bear right at the edge of a wood and go along a track with trees on the right and a hedge on the left. Go past houses and take the path bearing left downhill through a covered hedgerow. At a T-junction of tracks turn right and go ahead, ignoring a path coming in on the right. The sandy surface ends and a metalled road leads by a house on the right. Take the right turn signed for Hollybush Cottage, passing Hollybush Bungalow on your right.

As the track bends sharply right, keep left along the grassy path and at a T-junction of tracks turn right to reach a road. Go right, then left. Budworth Pool and the village soon come into view and the route descends gently to a stile on the right signposted for

Budworth Mere. Cross the stile and two further stiles ahead, then walk left around the pool. A stile will bring you on to a road: turn right into Little Budworth. At the church turn right – the Red Lion is on the left. About $^1/_2$ mile further along this road you will regain Church Lane passing the War Memorial and the Egerton Arms on the right. Continue to **Little Budworth Country Park** and the entrance to **Oulton Park**. Return to your car.

POINTS OF INTEREST:

Little Budworth Country Park – An area of ancient heath land, with poor, sandy soil. The Old Coach Road cuts through the common and horse riding is allowed on the west side only.

Oulton Park – Was a US Army camp during World War II, then a Polish Refugee camp. The original Hall burnt down in 1925 with only Old Lodge Gates, now an entrance to the racing track, surviving.

REFRESHMENTS:

The Red Lion, Little Budworth (tel no: 082 921 275). Varied bar meals served from 1.00pm-2.00pm; also separate family dining room. No dogs.

The Egerton Arms, Little Budworth (tel no: 082 921 250). Bar snacks on Saturdays and Sundays only. Children welcome. Dogs must be on a lead.

Walk 53   FARNDON AND THE RIVER DEE   3m (5km)

Maps: OS Sheets Landranger 117; Pathfinder SJ 45/55.

A short, easy walk through fields and along the banks of the River Dee.

Start: At 412545 on the Farndon side of Dee bridge.

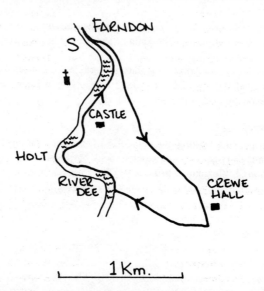

Walk down to the bridge and turn left immediately before it on to the river bank. Against a rock face, to your left, is a flight of stone steps which climb up behind the Boathouse Restaurant to reach an enclosed path. This path opens out beyond some houses and then becomes enclosed again as it nears a stile. Go over and bear left to a gate. Go over a cross track and a plank over a ditch, and skirt left round a small mound. To the right you can see **St Chad's Church** in Holt on the other side of the river.

The river begins to wind away from you at this point but you carry on over a field, with a hedge surrounding a filter bed to your right, aiming for a stile on the left. Go over and cross the track beyond. Go over a new road and up the bank to a waymarked stile. Go over another track and two further stiles, the second of which is also waymarked. After this quick succession of stiles go over the field ahead to a stile in front of you. On

112

the other side cross a field with a pond to the left and a row of poplars over to the right. Cross a stile and bear right in the next field to reach a corner stile. Go over to reach another 10 yards along in the right-hand hedge. Go over into a very large field, and you turn left and keep to the left-hand hedge. Stay with it until you see a white house among the trees ahead and slightly right. Go across the field using the house as a marker and leave through the right-hand opening on to a wide, well-defined track. Turn right and follow the track for 500 yards. When the route takes you through a field opening keep with the hedge on the right until you reach the river. Here a Public Footpath sign points the way to the right. Continue along the river to a stile. Go over to a clear path running high above the river. It passes under the new road and also by a small sandy bay. The banks are full of wild flowers in summer and on the far side of the river you can see the **Castle remains**. The route reaches a stile leading to a hedged-in path, but be wary of one or two gaps on the left where there are drops to the river. After a short distance you arrive back at the bridge and the starting point.

POINTS OF INTEREST:

St Chad's Church, Holt – Was extensively restored in 1732. The Parish Registers date back to the 1540s and the font to 1490. There are bullet marks inside the church testifying to fighting within its walls during the Civil War.

The Castle remains – Believed to be the site of a Roman fortress. The Norman castle was started about 1281 and suffered damage during the Civil War.

REFRESHMENTS:

The Boathouse Restaurant, Farndon (tel no: 0829 270430). Open Saturdays and Sundays from 12.00pm-6.00pm for snacks and sandwiches, tea and scones.

The Nag's Head, Farndon (tel no: 0829 2702671). Bar snacks and hot meals daily between 12.00pm and 2.00pm. Can only take children over 14. Dogs allowed.

Walk 54   SAIGHTON AND BRUERA   3m (5km)

Maps: OS Sheets Landranger 117; Pathfinder SJ 46/56.

A fairly level walk through farmland and a short stretch of woodland.

Start: At 443621, the parking place opposite the village school in Saighton.

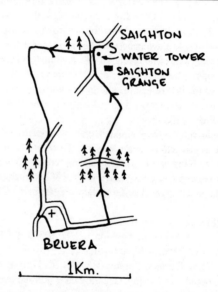

From the parking place, turn left and follow the road around a sharp bend. Opposite a prominent **square tower**, take a footpath on the right. Walk beside a plantation and where this ends climb over a fixed gate and continue ahead along a hedge. After 300 yards go through a small gate on your left. Keep ahead again, passing through several gates to reach a metalled road. Turn right and walk into the tiny hamlet of Bruera with its dominant **church**.

Turn left into the churchyard, passing to the right of the church. Near to a black hut the fence railings slide back allowing you through. Walk along the hedge to a gap opposite. Go through, over a footbridge and then cross a field. Turn left along the hedge (and not through the gap in it) and follow it to a stile. Go over on to a metalled road, turn right and after 300 yards take a footpath on your left, through a gate. Follow a hedge straight ahead. At the opposite end of the field climb over a fence and follow a row of trees to a gate opposite. Go through this into woodland, cross a private road (part of the Duke of Westminster's estate) and go into some more woodland. Go through to a gate with a footbridge beyond. Head straight across the next field making for the top left-hand corner where a footbridge crosses a small stream. Cross and bear right along the hedge to a metalled road at the southern edge of Saighton. To your right is the entrance to **Saighton Grange**. To return to the start, walk uphill back into the village.

POINTS OF INTEREST:

Square tower – This is a water tower, built in the 19th century to supply the village. A few years ago, it was used as the scene of several murders in a television detective series.

Bruera Church – This beautiful church, surrounded by ancient yew trees, is very old. The west wall, which is supported by immense buttresses, may date from Saxon times, while the rest of the church was built in the 12th century. In the south chapel are some interesting sculptures by the famous Nollekins of the 18th century.

Saighton Grange – Here once was the country house of the Abbots of Chester, of which only the embattled gatehouse, built in the 15th century, survives today. The magnificent house we now see, and the impressive gardens which surround it, were built for the second Marquess of Westminster in 1861.

Maps: OS Sheets Landranger 117; Pathfinder SJ 46/56.
A walk around the medieval walls of Chester.
Start: The George Street car park.

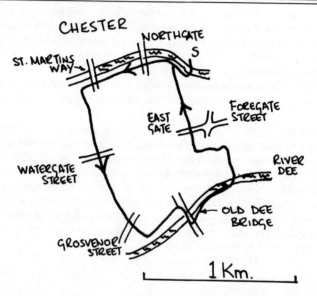

From the car park, turn left into George Street and then right into Frodsham Street. Go over the canal bridge and then right, down steps, on to the towpath of the Shropshire Union Canal. After 100 yards bear left through trees and up wooden steps on to the city wall. Turn right along the top of this, soon passing **King Charles Tower**, at the north-eastern corner of the city walls. Here the walls turn to the left, westwards. Below, running parallel, is the canal. Continue over Northgate and the recent St Martins Gate, which crosses the city ring road. At the north-western corner of the city walls is the **Water Tower**. The way turns southwards descending almost to street level. After crossing Watergate, on the right you can see Chester Racecourse known as the Roodee. Along this section, the top of the wall has become the street pavement. Beyond the Toll Office building, which houses Cheshire Constabulary, cross the city ring road into Castle Drive opposite which runs parallel to the River Dee. The imposing building to your left is **Chester Castle**. Soon you reach the old Dee Bridge. Leave the city walls here and cross this towards Handbridge. On the far side turn left beside the river, going past a weir, a restored water wheel and through parkland to the Queens Park suspension bridge. Just before going under this, bear right uphill and back over the Dee to the Chester side. Climb the steps opposite to St John's Church. Next to the church is an open area surrounded by low railings; go through the nearest gate and descend wooden steps to the **Roman Amphitheatre**. Leave on the opposite side and make for Newgate. On your left are the **Roman Gardens**. Go under Newgate and turn left. Almost immediately go through an arch on your left and up steps back on to the wall. Cross Newgate walking now between shops and other buildings. Cross over Eastgate to emerge into the parkland surrounding **Chester Cathedral**. A further 400 yards will bring you to steps back down to the canal towpath. Retrace your steps to the car park.

POINTS OF INTEREST:

King Charles Tower – According to tradition Charles I stood here to watch the defeat of his forces at the Battle of Rowton Moor in 1645. It was formerly called the Phoenix Tower and replaced the north-east tower of the old roman fortress. Today it houses an exhibition of the Civil War in Chester.

The Water Tower – Build in 1322, to guard the Port of Chester, when the river flowed right up to the city walls. It now contains an exhibition of medieval Chester.

Chester Castle – This was built in 1789, replacing the old medieval castle of which only the 13th-century Agricola Tower survives.

St John's Church – This was the old cathedral of Chester (1075–1102). It was built at the beginning of the 12th century by the first Norman Bishop of Mercia, and, as the ruins show, it was once much bigger than it is today.

The Roman Amphitheatre and Roman Gardens – This is the largest yet discovered in Britain, an oval arena measuring 190ft by 162ft, with seating for 7,000 people. Nearby are the Roman Gardens, with a reconstructed underfloor heating chamber or hypocaust.

Chester Cathedral – Dedicated to St Werburgh, whose remains lie in the Lady Chapel. Most of the building dates from between 1250 and 1538, when it was a Benedictine Abbey. It became a cathedral in 1541.

REFRESHMENTS:
Numerous within the city.

Walks 56 and 57 **NANTWICH AND THE RIVER WEAVER** 3m (5km)
Maps: OS Sheets Landranger 118; Pathfinder SJ 65/75.
A walk through Nantwich and on surfaced paths by the river.
Start: The Crown Hotel in High Street on the north side of the
Square in Nantwich.

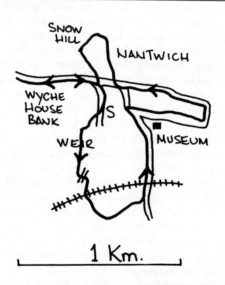

Turn away from the Square towards Oat Market passing the Union Inn, an 18th-century coaching inn, on the right. Go straight ahead, between Manweb and Kwiksave, enter the car park and keep to the right side of road. Pass by the modern swimming baths on your left and the **Old Outdoor Brine Baths**, built in 1883, next to them. At the end of these buildings turn left towards the River Weaver and left again before the footbridge to follow the river back towards the town. At traffic lights turn right over a bridge into Welsh Row. Go past The Three Pigeons, once a cock-fighting inn and with a mounting block standing outside, and the **Cheshire Cat** next door. Continue past Marsh Lane, which comes in on the left, to Malthouse Cottage, mentioned in a late 18th-century rating lists. You can now see the Shropshire Union Canal bridge spanning the road further on and an extension of the walk can be made from here in that direction to include **Dorfold Hall** about 800 yards further on. Return to the river bridge on the opposite side as you walk back. Turn right at the bridge and right again in 50 yards, by a paved area to cross the river. Carry on towards the houses ahead, go over a small bridge and turn left. Bear half-left to cross a further bridge and go immediately right, under the railway bridge, and follow the path to the **Grave of Lieutenant Brown**. Continue with the path until it comes out into Shrewbridge Road and cross over to a drive which has **Brookfield House** on the right and a children's playground on the left. The drive narrows as it runs between two houses fronting on to Wellington Road. In the garden of a house on the left is a small brick building which used to be a **School**. Turn left into Wellington Road, go over the level-crossing then straight ahead over the roundabout into Pillory Street. Half-way down on the left and set back from the road is a chapel of the Society of Friends, now converted into a theatre for the Nantwich Players. Between the chapel and the road was the site of the old town pillory. **Nantwich Museum**, once the Public Library, is on the opposite side of the road. Continue for another 150 yards along Pillory Street and then turn right into Hospital Street. About 250 yards up on the left is **Sweetbriar Hall**, a distinctive black and white building. As you move away from the town centre, past a mini roundabout, notice some fine old properties, many of which still retain medieval features. By a second, larger, roundabout you will find **Churche's Mansion** on the right which is both a restaurant and a house open to the public. Turn left here along the road to Chester and left again beyond the garage down South Crofts, turning right at the end and then immediately left into Monk's Lane. On your right are **Dysart Buildings** and half-way along on the left is The Bowling Green where you can get refreshments. Monk's Lane brings you out on the north (churchyard) side of **St Mary's Church**, and into the Square again. Turn right along High Street back to the **Crown Hotel**.

POINTS OF INTEREST:
Nantwich has an almost entirely Elizabethan centre, the result of a fire which devastated the town in 1583. Destroying all but three of the town's main buildings, the fire raged for twenty days. Sweetbriar Hall, Churche's Mansion and the parish church of St Mary were the three survivors, and each is passed on this route.

Following the fire Elizabeth I donated £2,000 and organised a nationwide collection, raising £30,000, a vast sum for the time, to finance the rebuilding of the town.

In gratitude, one new house, Queen's Aid House in The Square, was inscribed:

> *'God grant our Ryal Queen*
> *In England longe to Raign*
> *For she hath put her helping*
> *Hand to bild this town againe.'*

Many of the buildings in Nantwich are worth a moment of your time, but the following are, in the author's opinion, outstanding.

The Old Outdoor Brine Baths – An ancient brine spring near the River Weaver bridge provided the brine for the open-air swimming pool. The present bridge on Welsh Row was built in 1803 and replaced a former stone bridge which became unsafe.

The Cheshire Cat – Originally known as the Widows' Almshouse in the 17th century, it is now a discotheque.

Dorfold Hall – Built in 1616 the fine Hall is open Thursdays and Bank Holiday Mondays 2.00pm-5.00pm April to October, or by appointment. Tel no: 0270 625245.

The Grave of Lieutenant Brown – Lt Leslie Brown of the US Air Force crashed his Thunderbolt fighter here in January 1944. It is believed that he stayed with his plane when it got into difficulties rather than bailing out and allowing it to crash on the town.

Brookfield House – Built in the mid-19th century by a local businessman as a private residence. It later became the Urban District Council offices and is now a residential home.

School – Opened as a school in 1886 by James Hall, author of *A History of the Town and Parish of Nantwich*. The school closed in 1906.

Nantwich Museum – Permanent displays include exhibits on the salt and leather industries. Open 10.30am–4.30pm Monday–Saturday, April–September, including Bank Holidays. Closed Wednesday and Sunday. October–March also closed on Mondays.

Sweetbriar Hall – Built in 1450 as a private residence, this has occasionally been used as a school. Now used as private offices. The Hall was one of the few buildings to escape the Great Fire of 1583.

Churche's Mansion – An Elizabethan mansion built in 1577 which also escaped the Great Fire. The restaurant is on the ground floor and the upper floor, open to view during the summer months, is furnished in the style of a late 16th-century mansion.

Dysart Buildings – Georgian houses built in the 18th century by the 2nd Earl of Dysart. All the houses are Grade II listed.

The Parish Church of St Mary – Dates from 1133. Unusual features include the ribbed vault in the chancel and the stalls, believed to have been made around 1390, of which each seat is carved out of a single trunk.

The Crown Hotel – This was erected in 1585, after the Great Fire. While the parish church was being used as a prison in the Civil War, the Crown was used as a place of worship.

REFRESHMENTS:

The Bowling Green Inn, The Gullet (tel no: 0270 626001). Serves bar snacks and also hot meals. Open 12.00pm–2.00pm Monday–Friday, 12.00–2.30pm Sunday and 12.00pm–9.00pm Saturday. Children welcome. Dogs not allowed when food is being served.

The Lamb Hotel, Hospital Street (tel no: 0270 625286). Bar snacks and bistro menu daily 12.00pm–2.00pm and 6.00pm–10.00pm. Also restaurant service. Children and well-behaved dogs welcome.

Churche's Mansion, Hospital Street (tel no: 0270 625933). Full afternoon tea served daily 2.30pm–4.00pm. Restaurant does 3-course lunches and dinner in the evening. Children welcome but dogs not allowed.

Walk 58   **MARBURY AND BIG MERE**   3¼m (6km)

Maps: OS Sheets Landranger 117; Pathfinder SJ 44/54.

An easy walk in picturesque countryside.

Start: At 554459, next to a footpath sign on the road to Wirswall.

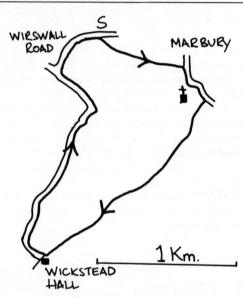

Cross a stile by the gate on the left and go across the field keeping the ditch on your right.
At the far corner bear left to a stile. Go over and follow a ditch to the far side of the field.
Cross a small footbridge, then a large farm bridge. Follow the right edge of a field to
the side of the mere then bear left to walk uphill to a gate and stile on the right. Cross
here, then go diagonally left to a road junction. Turn right and walk along the road to
the village of Marbury. Just before the Swan Inn turn right into a drive leading to **St
Michael's Church**. Leave the churchyard by a gate under the **Old Gnarled Elm**.

Go downhill to a stile. Cross the lane and turn right for a short distance to another
stile signed for Wirswall. Walk to Big Mere, then walk left beside the water crossing
two stiles close together, then another at the end of the mere. There are lovely views
back across the water to St Michael's Church from this section. Walk with trees on
your left to an iron fence below a solitary house. Go through a gate and bear right to

walk through the grassy hollow ahead. At the end of the hollow go through a gate and cross to the hillside above.

Climb the slope, bearing slightly left, and cross a field to a small gate in the hedge. Wickstead Hall stands behind trees on top of the hill. Walk up the field aiming to the right of the Hall to a point where a hedge meets an iron fence. Cross a stile here and continue up, with a hedge on your left, to reach a stile. Go over on to a lane, go right and downhill for 1 mile back to your car.

POINTS OF INTEREST:

St Michael's Church – An attractive little church which was first mentioned in 1299. Imaginative gargoyles have been set into the outer walls, and inside, the pulpit, which was carved in the 15th century, is well worth seeing. The church is suffering from subsidence.

Old Gnarled Elm – Local legend states that if this elm, reputed to be 1,000 years old, falls then the church itself will fall into the mere. Parishioners have guarded against this by placing a chain around the tree.

REFRESHMENTS:

The Swan Inn (tel no: 0948 3715). An historic pub in a scenic position. It is welcoming towards walkers and is proud of its menu which includes, besides snacks and meals, a wide choice of interesting desserts.

Walk 59   LARKTON HILL AND BICKERTON $3^1/_4$m (6km)

Maps: OS Sheets Landranger 117; Pathfinder SJ 45/55.

A straightforward walk with lovely views across the Cheshire plain.

Start: At 494535, the small car park below Larkton Hill.

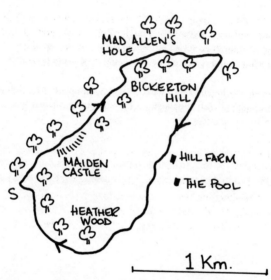

Walk uphill following the direction of the Sandstone Trail signed for Bickerton, Rawhead and Beeston. At the crest of the rise turn right and climb the steep but sound path past numerous wild bilberry bushes. Rocky steps bring you to **Maiden Castle** at the top.

Turn left and follow the path above the escarpments, which offers excellent viewpoints. Descend through trees to an open area where a footpath sign indicates Brown Knowl and Copper Mine Inn to the left. Ignore this and walk on for 50 yards to another sign and follow it left towards Rawhead. Walk around another section of escarpment, then drop downhill past **Mad Allen's Hole** and continue down to reach a stile. Go over and cross to the road almost opposite **Holy Trinity Church**.

Leave the Sandstone Trail here, turn right along the lane and follow it for $^3/_4$ mile, past Hill Farm on your left and The Pool on your right, to reach Larkton Cottage. Turn right on to the footpath signposted 'Larkton Hill, Sandstone Trail'. Walk between two banks, then continue with a sandstone wall on your left along the edge of the wood. You will shortly rejoin the Sandstone Trail. Soon after this the path forks. It is best to choose the lower path signposted 'No Horses Please'. Follow this path till you rejoin the Larkton Hill track and are able to turn left to rejoin your car.

POINTS OF INTEREST:

Maiden Castle – The remains of an Iron Age hill fort last occupied about 2,000 years ago. There is a single entrance guarded by two defensive banks and ditches.

Mad Allen's Hole – A small outcrop of sandstone by the path. It is unclear how it gained its unusual name, but modern visitors have left their personal marks scratched in the soft rock.

Holy Trinity Church – Originally a 'chapel of ease', built for local parishioners who found it difficult to travel to their parish church at Malpas, 7 miles away.

REFRESHMENTS:

These two inns are situated opposite each other by the Broxton roundabout, where the A41 crosses the A534.

The Broxton Hall Country House Hotel and Restaurant (tel no: 082 925 321). Basically an 'up market' establishment but snacks are available in the bar lounge.

The Egerton Arms (tel no: 082 925 241). Provides a good range of bar meals with a daily 'chef's special'. There is also a beer garden and an à la carte restaurant.

Walk 60　　HAUGHTON MOSS AND BUNBURY　　3¹⁄₄m (6km)

Maps: OS Sheets Landranger 117; Pathfinder SJ 45/55.

A level walk through farmland but with hilly lanes in Bunbury village.

Start: At 578564, near a junction of lanes in Haughton Moss.

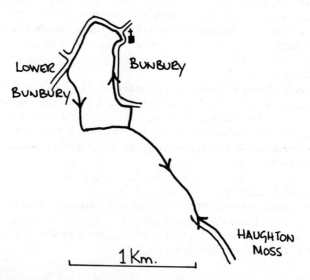

Follow the lane signed as a No Through Road past Ferret Oak Farm on the right to reach a stile on the left of a gate ahead. Go over, bear slightly right across a field and cross a footbridge over a stream. Walk ahead, go over another stile and cross a large field towards a line of telegraph poles crossing your path at right angles. From here there is a view of Beeston Castle and the tower of Bunbury Church. Go over the stile in the hedge beyond the telegraph poles and follow the hedge on the right. A gate to the left of a field opening leads into a small field. Go through a gate on the far side, cross another field to a third gate and go through on to a narrow hedged-in path. Follow this path for a short way and cross a stile on the right. Follow the row of trees on the right, going over three make-shift stiles. Beyond the third stile walk diagonally left across a field towards a group of houses and a stile in the corner. Go over and turn left along a lane, passing the Methodist Church on the right, and then turn right into Bunbury. Continue past the Nag's Head, where they serve food at the weekends, along Vicarage Lane and up the hill to **St Boniface's Church.** The Dysart Arms is opposite the church and has food every day.

Take Wyche Lane leading downhill to the right in front of the church and continue for about $1/2$ mile, keeping to the left where another lane joins it. Just after a left-hand bend in the lane there is a signpost for Haughton on the right. Follow this track and when you reach a field turn immediately left over a stile. This brings you into the field with the telegraph poles at right angles to the path which you originally came over. Retrace your steps over the footbridge past Ferret Oak Farm and so down the lane to where the car is parked.

POINTS OF INTEREST:

The Parish Church of St Boniface, Bunbury – Dates back to the 14th and 15th century and possesses a rare alabaster effigy to Sir Hugh Calveley who died in 1394. A double drained piscina was discovered in the 19th century when whitewash was removed from the walls and more recently during restoration the figure of an angel was found on the north side of the east window. There is a 17th-century octagonal font with an unusual oak cover.

REFRESHMENTS:

The Nag's Head, Bunbury (tel no: 0829 260265). Meals and snacks Saturdays and Sundays only. Children and dogs welcome.

The Dysart Arms, Bunbury (tel no: 0829 260183). Home-cooked dishes and snacks every day. Unable to accommodate children. No dogs.

Walk 61 CHESTER CITY WALLS AND THE MEADOWS 4m (6.5km)

Maps: OS Sheets Landranger 117; Pathfinder SJ 46/56.

Level stone on the walls and flat walking on The Meadows

Start: The clock in Eastgate Street.

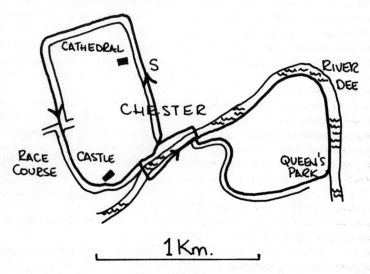

Ascend the walls at the Eastgate Clock by the steps between the Midland Bank and Burtons. Turn right at the top, away from the clock and a few yards on there is a good view of Chester Cathedral (see Walk 55) on the left. King Charles' Tower (see Walk 55) stands where the walls go left and as you walk above Northgate Street and the Inner Ring Road, the Shropshire Union Canal runs immediately below on the right. From the Water Tower you can see, to the north, three locks used by the Chester and Ellesmere canals and the River Dee. The walls now bridge the railway line and beyond are ramps leading down to street level and, shortly, back up again. Continue with **Chester Racecourse** on your right until you reach the lights in Grosvenor Road from where you can see the continuation of the walls beyond the bollards on the opposite side of the road. The Castle (see Walk 55) is now above you on the left. Keep left with the walls and descend by a ramp to cross a road with wide grass verges. Stay left for a few yards to reach the end of the **Old Dee Bridge** opposite Bridgegate, one of the city's main gates. Go over the bridge and down steps on the left to the river bank. Pass the Weir, built to provide water power for mills in the 11th century, and the **Suspension Bridge**, where there is a good view of Grosvenor Park on the opposite bank with rows of mainly 19th century houses leading down to the waterfront. Go through a gate on to grass and after about $1/_3$ mile you will reach an opening with a stile. Immediately before this turn right and, keeping the brook on your left, you will come to a stile, also on the left. Go over into Bottoms Lane and on into St George's Crescent. Follow the crescent round to the right as far as its junction with Queen's Park Road. Turn right and immediately left into Victoria Crescent. This crescent weaves left and after about 300 yards there is a short road downhill on the right leading to the suspension bridge. Go over and turn left along the promenade where there are several 19th century kiosks and a bandstand. When you reach Old Dee Bridge climb back on to the walls by the steps to the right across Bridge Street. Continue until you see the Albion Inn, an old Victorian corner pub, on your left. There are steps down should you wish to reach it, otherwise continue. for a short distance to reach the Eastgate Clock once more. From the bridge there is a good view of the Roman Watling Street, now Eastgate Street to the west and Foregate Street to the east. Go down the steps into Eastgate Street to finish.

POINTS OF INTEREST:

Chester Racecourse – Situated on the Roodee, originally used for grazing, recreation and as a training ground for soldiers. One of the oldest racecourses in the country.
The Old Dee Bridge – The only bridge in Chester until the 19th century, this was originally part timber, part stone.
Suspension Bridge – Erected in 1852 to connect Queen's Park, a new suburb, to Chester and rebuilt in 1923.

REFRESHMENTS:

Numerous available in the city.
The Albion Inn, corner of Park Street and Albion Street (tel no: 0244 40345). CAMRA *Good Beer Guide* and Which *Good Pubs Guide*. Open daily 12.00pm–1.45pm. Reasonable prices and comprehensive menu including Indian dishes. Children welcome but dogs allowed in bar only.

Walk 62   ACTON TO SWANLEY   4m (6.5km)

Maps: OS Sheets Landranger 118; Pathfinder SJ 65/75.

Flat, easy walking but muddy in places.

Start: At 632531, park opposite Acton church.

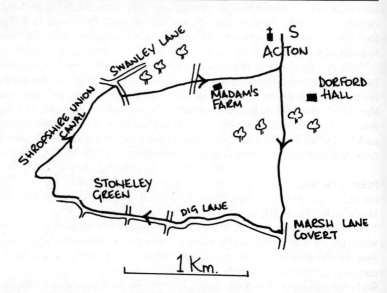

Turn right after leaving the car and right again on to the A51. Go past the Star Inn to reach a signpost for Marsh Lane. The signed bridleway is about 1 mile long and to the left of it lies **Dorfold Hall**, while Beeston Hills can be seen in the opposite direction. Turn right down Dig Lane, a metalled lane with high hedges. Go over at the crossroads to a short straight lane which leads to another crossroads. Carry straight on past houses until the lane turns right on to a track. Go through the gate ahead. The next section can be muddy, as you follow the hedge on the left round a sharp corner to reach another gate. Go through to a small meadow and cross it to a bridge over the Shropshire Union Canal.

Just before the bridge, on the right, is a stile leading to the towpath. Go over and turn right for about $^1/_2$ mile passing by a small lock and going under a bridge. Look out for wood anemones, lesser celandine and violets which can be found on the banks of the canal. At the next bridge leave the towpath and take the middle road signposted for

Chester and Nantwich. Between some houses and a plantation about 200 yards down the road take a track to the right. After 25 yards the plantation ends and you bear left into a field. Although from the map the path goes across the field at an angle, it is probably easier to keep left with the fence and plantation on your immediate left and follow the hedge round to the right at the end of the field. At a large gap in the hedge (there is a gatepost) turn left into a field and head straight across it, with telegraph poles coming in on the right and a pond and clump of trees on the left, to join the road. If you look to your left here you will see a **Windmill** with a wind-pump on top and, a little to the right, **Acton Church**.

Directly opposite you will see a waymarker pointing up the drive of Madam's Farm. Follow this and where the drive bends right, go ahead to cross a stile and into a field. Go straight over this field to a rusty iron kissing gate in the metal fence ahead. Keeping the church to the left, walk ahead to another kissing gate, ignoring a track going away on your left. Beyond the gate bear left and head for a group of trees in the top left-hand corner of the next field. Here you join the track where the walk started and return to the car by taking the left turn after passing the Star Inn.

POINTS OF INTEREST:

Dorfold Hall – Built in 1616 by Ralph Wilbraham. The Drawing Room has a fine Jacobean ceiling. The garden has a Spanish Chestnut over 1,000 years old. Hall open Tuesdays and Bank Holiday Mondays 2.00pm–5.00pm April–October.

Windmill – The brickwork is late 18th century and the walls are 5 bricks thick. It ground corn until the late 1880s. In 1890 the sails were replaced by a windpump and the mill became a water tower supplying the **Dorfold Estate**.

St Mary's Church, Acton – Dates mainly from the 13th and 14th centuries. It contains carved stones from the late 11th century and a 12th-century font.

REFRESHMENTS:

The Star Inn, Acton (tel no: 0270 627296). Sandwiches and rolls daily 12.00pm–3.00pm. Older children welcome. Dogs in bar only.

A mile further down the road in Nantwich there are pubs, cafés and wine bars serving refreshments.

Walk 63 BEESTON CASTLE AND THE PECKFORTON WOODS 4$\frac{1}{2}$m (7.5km)

Maps: OS Sheets Landranger 117; Pathfinder SJ 45/55.

An easy walk with a short uphill climb.

Start: At 540592, the car park outside Beeston Castle.

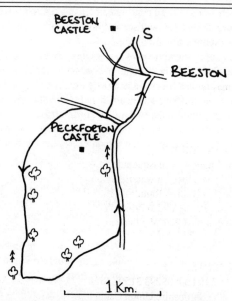

From the car park turn left and follow the lane for 30 yards to reach a footpath on the right at another small car park. The way is marked by a Sandstone Trail emblem and a signpost to Rawhead and Bickmerton. Continue through a small conifer plantation. Cross a stile and a lane and follow a path across a maize field. From here there are fine views of **Peckforton Castle** ahead and **Beeston Castle** behind.

Descend wooden steps, cross a small bridge and stile, and follow the edge of a field with a fence on the right. Cross a stile and bear right along the lane. After 400 yards turn left through a gate into the Peckforton Estate. If the track between the two banks is muddy an easier path may be found up on the right bank. After about 1 mile you will reach a footpath crossroads. Continue ahead but shortly leave the main track and bear left up a path which leads steeply up through the wood. At the top bear right and go

132

through a kissing gate. Follow a stone wall on the left and cross a stile. Turn left along a lane to two sandstone cottages and turn left at the lane junction near them.

At this point we leave the Sandstone Trail and continue along the lane between a house and outbuildings. The lane becomes a track which curves to the right and drops gently downhill through a wood to a small sandstone bridge. Bear right here, follow the cobbled track for 50 yards and go through a steel gate. Bear left at the junction and after ten yards ascend the bank on the right. (*Care should be taken not to miss this ascent.*) Cross three stiles then follow a path across a barley field. Cross two stiles on to a road and bear left. Follow the road, past the imposing Victorian Gothic gatehouse to the Peckforton Estate, to reach a small lane joining your road on the left. Here you may turn left and follow the lane for 30 yards to reach a stile on the right which marks the point where you may retrace your steps back to Beeston Castle. Alternatively, continue along the road to Beeston village and turn left at the old school (now an Outdoor Education Centre) and follow this lane back to Beeston Castle.

POINTS OF INTEREST:

Peckforton Castle – A masquerade fortress, built in 1844 for Lord Tollemache. It contains real gatehouses, a waterless moat and a Great Hall with a raised dais.

Beeston Castle – Built by Ranulf III, Earl of Chester, in 1220, perhaps to help to secure his friendship with the Welsh Prince Llywelyn. It was a Parliamentarian stronghold at the beginning of the Civil War but was captured in a surprise night attack by just nine bold Royalists.

REFRESHMENTS:

The Shady Oak (tel no: 08293 3159). Situated $^1/_2$ mile from Beeston Castle where the lane crosses the Shropshire Union Canal near Wharton's Lock, this inn offers a good range of food in pleasant surroundings. A children's play area is provided.

Snack bar, in the second car park. This provides tea, coffee and light snacks during the summer months.

Walk 64   MALPAS AND OVERTON HEATH   4³/₄m (8km)

Maps: OS Sheets Landranger 117; Pathfinder SJ 44/54.

A delightful walk which begins in one of Cheshire's oldest villages.

Start: At 487477, the car park in Malpas village centre opposite the Fire Station.

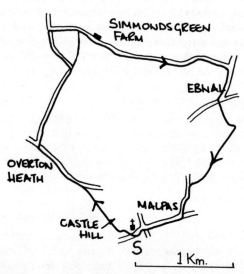

Turn left out of the car park and walk down to the crossroads where the Thurlow Memorial stands. Turn right and walk up the quaint old street into the grounds of the **Church of St Oswald**, which is well worth a visit.

After leaving the church, turn right and walk towards the gate with a light over it. Where the path forks, go right up three steps and walk on past a large mound on your right, which is all that remains of **Malpas Castle**. Go between hedges, then cross a small lane and continue through a wooden gate. Follow a path, to a stile, go over and walk across the facing field. There are magnificent views from here across the Cheshire Plain to the Clwydian Hills of Wales. Go through a kissing gate and step down to a narrow lane. Turn left and walk downhill through the hamlet of Overton Heath. Follow

134

the lane as it bears sharp right and climbs uphill. At the next bend continue straight ahead up the track past Alport Farm. This track may be wet after about 400 yards but it is possible to step through a gap in the hedge on the left and to continue along the edge of the field.

Continue to a bridleway on the left, signposted 'No Through Road for Motor Vehicles'. Take the bridleway and descend through a wood and past small outcrops of sandstone to emerge at a road. Turn right and go straight ahead at a staggered crossroads, passing Simmonds Green Farm and following this pleasant lane for about 1 mile. At a T-junction, go right uphill past a farm. Just after the gate into the farmyard you will see a stile on your left. Go over this then through the gate on the left. Bear right and follow the track to a facing gate and stile. Cross here and follow the fence on your left. Turn right before the next gate and walk ahead under the power lines, following their course. Malpas church will be seen on the hilltop before you. Cross a track using two stiles then follow the facing track between two hedges. Join a farm track and walk down it to a lane. Turn left along the lane, then bear right at a junction and right again at the next junction. Walk past the telephone box, then go uphill, back to the centre of Malpas.

POINTS OF INTEREST:

The Church of St Oswald, Malpas – Built in the 14th century. It has an unusual sundial over the door and there is a 13th-century iron-clad chest just inside the door. In the chapel is an alabaster effigy of Sir Randle Brereton, a local man who served Henry VII and Henry VIII.

Malpas Castle – A pre-conquest 'motte and bailey' which guarded the important road down the Welsh border.

REFRESHMENTS:

The Red Lion, Malpas (tel no: 0948 860368). A 12th-century inn at Malpas crossroads which offers, for the modern traveller, bar snacks and meals – and a sauna and solarium! *The Old Vaults*, Malpas (tel no: 0948 860245). Offers a good selection of meals including vegetarian dishes. Situated opposite the church.

Walk 65   GUILDEN SUTTON AND CHRISTLETON   5m (8km)

Maps: OS Sheets Landranger 117; Pathfinder SJ 46/56.

An easy walk through fields and across a golf course.

Start: At 449683, the Guilden Sutton car park.

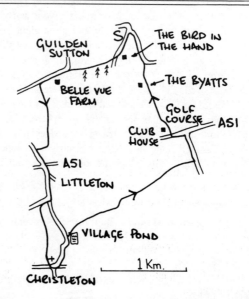

From the car park turn right, passing The Bird in the Hand. Just beyond the pub turn right through a kissing gate and go up some steps between trees. At the top go through another kissing gate on to a metalled footpath at the rear of some houses. Follow this path, keeping woodland on your left, to emerge between houses into Belle Vue Lane on a sharp bend. Go ahead and after 400 yards a wide farm track beside the orchard of Belle Vue Farm. Follow the track past a house and then bear slightly right into a passageway hedged on one side by conifers. Cross a stile at the end of this and a hedge. On the far side of the field, cross another stile and turn right on to a lane. The lane reaches a metalled road. Turn left along the road to its junction with the A51. Go straight across this into the village of Littleton. Do not go into the centre of the village, but keep right towards Christleton. Turn right into Pearl Lane and after 200 yards take a footpath on your left over a stile. Follow a well-defined footpath towards Christleton Church, crossing two fields. A stile leads into a passageway beside the church. Follow this to the main street of **Christleton**.

Turn left along Pepper Street with its many attractive Georgian-style houses. At the village green turn left again and pass **The Old Hall** on your right. Continue to the large village pond, a beautiful spot and a haven for all sorts of wildlife and birds. Just past the pond take a footpath on the right. Where this forks, bear right and go around a house and through a gap. Bear right here along a hedge and through two gateways to a stile. Go over and follow a hedge. Go past a pond, then over a footbridge and through a gap in the hedge. Keep straight ahead, then bear slightly left to cross another stile. Bear slightly left again to reach a metalled road. Turn left along this to its junction with the A51. Cross and turn left towards Chester.

After about 200 yards take a footpath on the right beside a golf clubhouse. Bear left around the back of this and then turn right beside some trees and the 1st tee. Keep ahead along the edge of the fairway, cross a brook and go up a wooded fringe between two more fairways. Beyond a green, cross a fairway to the hedge opposite and a sign marked 'stile'. Go over the stile to a field and go across to another stile. Go through a small kitchen garden to a track beside a farmyard. After crossing a cattlegrid, take the lane ahead. At the next junction bear left into Guilden Sutton. At the junction in the centre of the village, where the road swings to the right, turn left to return to the car park.

POINTS OF INTEREST:

Christleton – This large, sprawling village is full of interesting and impressive houses, dating from the mid-17th century onwards. Christleton Hall has its own gazebo, an unusual summerhouse built into the garden wall, so that the ladies of the house could watch coaches going by.

The Old Hall, Christleton – This dates from about 1605 and is the oldest building in the village. During the Siege of Chester in the Civil War, which lasted 6 months, this was probably the headquarters of the Parliamentarian forces. There is also a local tradition that the tunnel which encircles the whole building was at one time linked with Chester.

REFRESHMENTS:

The Bird in the Hand, Guilden Sutton (tel no: 0244 300341).
The Ring O Bells, Christleton (tel no: 0244 332244).

Walk 66   NANTWICH, HURLESTON AND ACTON   5m (8km)

Maps: OS Sheets Landranger 118; Pathfinder SJ 65/75.

A walk of interest to those who value our industrial heritage.

Start: At 643527, the aqueduct in Nantwich just beyond Malbank School.

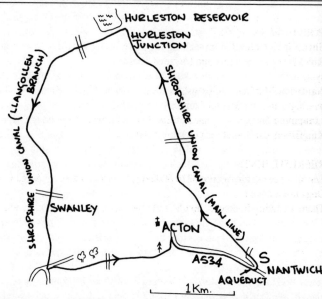

Climb the embankment by a flight of stairs to reach the **Shropshire Union Canal**. Go right along the towpath past **Nantwich Marina** and under the A51 to reach Hurleston Junction. Go left over the canal to join the **Llangollen Branch** of the Shropshire Union near a flight of four locks and a lock-keepers cottage. Continue along the towpath past Hurleston Reservoir. Just beyond an overhead pipeline and a lock you reach Swanley Bridge on the Acton road. Leave the canal towpath at this point and turn left down Swanley Lane in the direction of Acton for 100 yards to a footpath sign on the right. The entrance to the path is blocked, so go through a gate a little further on and cross the field diagonally left to the right-hand edge of a plantation. Go straight across the next field to an open gateway in line with a three-storey farm. Continue toward the farm passing a pond on the left. Cross a minor road and enter the farm drive, keeping straight on where it bends to the right. Go over a stile and head across an open field to the next boundary and the remains of an old gate. Go over the gate and continue in the same direction to the next field boundary and the remains of another old gate. Go over this and diagonally left to the top left corner of a field and a driveway. Go left over a cattlegrid for 100 yards to meet the A534. About 100 yards left is the Star Inn and Acton Church (see Walk 62). Go right and follow the footpath past Dorfold Hall (see Walk 62) for 1km to reach the aqueduct and the start point.

POINTS OF INTEREST:

Shropshire Union Canal – Designed and built by Thomas Telford and linking the River Dee and the Trent and Mersey Canals to the Midlands and the rest of the canal system.

Nantwich Marina – A British Waterways Marina with canal gift shop. A popular overnight stop for holiday barges.

Llangollen Branch – A spur of the 'Union' worth walking along its entire length. Kingfishers can sometimes be seen in the area.

REFRESHMENTS:

The Star Inn, Acton (tel no: 0270 627296). Bar snacks and meals. Children welcome. Dogs not allowed.

There are many fine pubs, hotels, and other eating places in Nantwich.

Walk 67 ASTON JUXTA MONDRUM AND BARBRIDGE 5$\frac{1}{2}$m (9km)

Maps: OS Sheets Landranger 118; Pathfinder SJ 65/75.
A friendly walk with easy route-finding.
Start: At 652568, by the church in Aston juxta Mondrum.

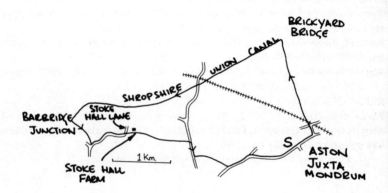

Facing the church go right (north-east) and take the metalled road on your left after a few hundred metres to a T-junction. Go over and take the gravelled lane to a stile. Go over and over a railway bridge to reach a lane. Go along the lane and over a field to reach the Middlewich Branch of the Shropshire Union Canal at Brickyard Bridge. Go over the bridge and left along the towpath for about 1 mile. The banks here are rich in wild flowers in the Spring. Just before the **Venetian Marina** the towpath improves considerably. Pass the Marina on the left and continue for about 1$\frac{1}{2}$ miles to **Barbridge Junction**.

Leave the Middlewich Branch of the canal at the junction and take the Wolverhampton Branch past the Barbridge pub to the bridge at Stoke Hall Lane. Access to the pub is over this bridge. Go left along the lane to reach Stoke Hall Farm at a left-hand bend. Follow a footpath sign to the right of the farm lane, going over a field and past the right side of a pond. Make for a stile to the left of a gate straight ahead, go over it and head across to a line of trees and a stream near where a hedgerow comes down from the opposite bank. Go through a gate and over two stiles, then turn left and follow a hedge on its right side. Go over another stile by a trig. point and turn right for a stile on to a road. Turn right for 150 yards to a footpath sign and stile on the left opposite a farm. Go over across a field and then over a series of stiles on to a road to the right of a large farm. Turn left past the farm to a fork in the road. Take the right fork to regain the start point.

POINTS OF INTEREST:

Venetian Marina – Here you will see an unbelievable array of water craft, demonstrating the popularity of canal boating, if you needed convincing.

Barbridge Junction – Near the Marina there is a strange radio telescope apparently left over from World War II, when there was a tracking station and aerodrome at nearby Wardle which played a part in the defence of Manchester.

REFRESHMENTS:

The Barbridge (tel no: 027 073 266). A pub with its own moorings and a large and well-equipped childrens' play area. Food, lunch and evenings, seven days a week. Children welcome, but please keep dogs on a lead.

Walk 68 GALLANTRY BANK AND BULKELEY HILL 5¹/₂m (9km)

Maps: OS Sheets Landranger 117; Pathfinder SJ 45/55.

A strenuous but rewarding walk through lovely countryside.

Start: At 517552, a lay-by on the right of the A534.

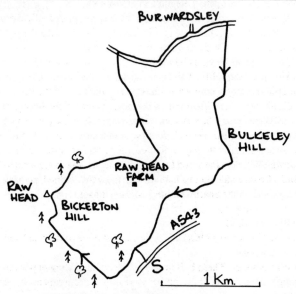

Go across the road and take the lane opposite until it bears to the right. Cross a stile to the left by a sign for the Sandstone Trail. Go downhill, cross a footbridge and climb some steps. Continue ahead to reach a footpath junction. Turn right along the path signposted 'Rawhead, Beeston'. At the top of a rise bear left into and through a wood. Beyond, the path is narrow and sandy and leads up over outcrops to the trig. point on **Rawhead**.

Follow the Sandstone Trail around the edge of the hill, then through woodland for about ¹/₂ mile, to reach a stile. Go over on to a track by The Bungalow. Just beyond is a stile on the left and a sign indicating 'Burwardsley'. Go over, walk under trees for 30 yards and then follow the fence on the left. Cross a stile on the left after 300 yards and walk downhill with a wire fence on your left. Cross the stile at the end of the field and go across the facing field in the direction indicated by the 'Burwardsley' sign. After 250 yards cross a small stile over an electric fence and walk on towards the middle of the wood ahead, where you will shortly see a white post marking a stile. Go over and through the small wood. Cross a footbridge and stile, then walk with a telegraph pole on your right. Follow a small stream until you are able to cross a stile on to a narrow lane. Turn right and walk uphill past Quarry House Farm, then between steep banks until the lane levels out by the **Cheshire Workshops**.

Drop downhill to a crossroads with the Pheasant Inn opposite. Turn right then after 30 yards turn left into the lane marked 'No Through Road'. Take the right-hand fork and continue steeply uphill. Look for a cottage on the right with the unusual name of Elephant Track. About 40 yards beyond is a stile on the right with a sign indicating 'Bulkeley Hill, Bickerton Hill'. This is the Sandstone Trail again. Go over the stile and follow the Trail crossing a number of stiles around the edge of the Peckforton Estate. Descend a bank into a lane. Turn left and then right and follow the sign for Bulkeley Hill. After 150 yards go up the steps on your left and follow the path through the wood to the top of Bulkeley Hill. The path goes beneath the trees, then through a gap in an iron fence. Bear right after the gap, walk under the concrete waterworks building, and continue downhill. Leave the wood by a gate where the way is signposted 'Rawhead, Larkton Hill'. Cross a stile on to a lane, turn left and follow the lane back to the start lay-by, recognised by the nearby **Copper Mine Chimney**.

POINTS OF INTEREST:

Rawhead – At 227 metres (746ft) this is the highest point of the Sandstone Trail, and an excellent viewpoint.

Cheshire Workshops – These buildings provide an interesting opportunity to watch candles being made by hand. These, and other examples of country crafts, are displayed for sale.

Copper Mine Chimney – This is the chimney for a copper mine pumping house which removed the water which had percolated through the sandstone into the mine. The mine was started in 1697 and was worked intermittently for about 200 years.

REFRESHMENTS:

The Bickerton Poacher (tel no: 082 922 226).
The Cheshire Workshops (tel no: 0829 70401). Offers snacks and soft drinks, and also has a licensed restaurant.

Walk 69   WHITCHURCH AND WIRSWALL   6m (9.5km)

Maps: OS Sheets Landranger 117; Pathfinder SJ 44/54.

An easy walk mainly on field paths although there could be route-finding difficulties. Map and compass essential!

Start: At 545415, the free car park in Whitchurch.

From the car park turn left along the A41 towards Chester. At a filling station, cross the road and take the path over the Recreation Ground. Go along Elizabeth Street, which is almost opposite, until it joins George Street. Turn left and 10 yards ahead is a Public Footpath sign. Go over the ladder and over two stiles ahead, then cross a bridge over a **dismantled railway**. Go over a stile and bear half-left towards a sycamore tree. Pass behind the tree and turn left at once over a stile on to a lane by a white house. Turn left almost immediately right over a stile where an arrow indicates the direction of the path up the rise beyond. Ahead is a golf course, reached where a rusty iron fence stands by the flimsy wire boundary. Head almost due north across the course. Just past the first green, in the far corner of the course there is a stile, to the right of a small pond and a copse. Go over this and another by a water trough. Ignore the farm track going left to right and aim for a facing stile with waymark arrows. Cross the field beyond, bearing slightly left, to a stile marking the boundary between Cheshire and Shropshire. Keep ahead over two fields separated by a stile, then go through a gate. Keep left along a hedge – although a detour to the trig. point on the slope to the right will reward you with fine views of Shropshire and mid-Wales. Go through a gate ahead and aim for the squat water tower. Bear right to a stile on to a farm track. Turn left to join a road, then left again into the parish of Wirswall.

After 300 yards turn right down a bridleway and after a further 150 yards follow a sign for the bridleway which turns sharp left. Descend, go through a gate and turn right with the bridleway signs. At a sharp right bend go forward through an iron gate. This part of the route can at times be overgrown with nettles, but as the path goes directly ahead it is possible to walk parallel to it in the right-hand field and rejoin it after passing a pond. Continue straight on until you come to the A49. Turn right and, after 40 yards, go left over a lock. Pass in front of the Willemoor Lock Tavern, where refreshments are available and continue along the canal towpath for 1 mile to cross Jackson's Bridge (No. 26). Go through a gate and keep left by a brook. Cross a stile in a corner and skirt left round a rise to a gate with yellow waymarkers, ignoring the white field gate. Keep left by a brook and follow it as it curves to the right. A stile in the hedge to the left leads to a footbridge. Go over and bear right to the next stile. Go over this, a footbridge and another stile. There is a further stile a little way ahead, but before it turn right and follow the fence on your left. Cross another stile in the top corner of the field, then keep to the edge of the field with the hedge on your right. A gap in this hedge gives access to the dismantled railway track. Go left for $^1/_4$ mile along the railway track then, 25 yards before a row of houses, turn right and across a field to a corner stile. Go over and left to reach the A49. Turn right, and at the roundabout follow the A41 signs to Wolverhampton to regain the start.

POINTS OF INTEREST:

Dismantled railway – This is the old local line from Whitchurch to Chester. Last passenger service in 1957. The line was closed in 1963.

REFRESHMENTS:

The Brownlow Restaurant, Whitchurch (tel no: 0948 2087). Opposite car park.
The Railway Inn, Whitchurch (tel no: 0948 2508). Opposite car park.

Walk 70   **AROUND WRENBURY**   6$^1/_2$m (10km)

Maps: OS Sheets Landranger 117; Pathfinder SJ 44/54.

*A delightful and rewarding walk which at the right times can be
rich in wildlife and wild flowers.*

Start: At 590481, Wrenbury Bridge.

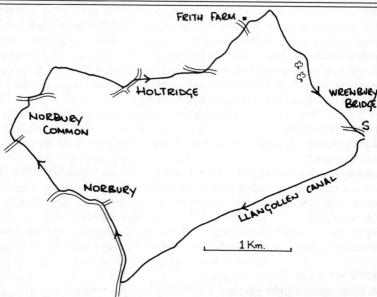

Follow the Llangollen Canal, a branch of the Shropshire Union Canal, westwards from
the Dusty Miller for 1$^1/_2$ miles with **Marbury Brook** on your left. The obelisk on the
left horizon is a monument in Combermere Park. At the first road bridge Church
Bridge, leave the canal and go right for Norbury. Go through the hamlet bearing left
and passing the **Garden of Models** on your right. Take a footpath on the right after 150
yards through a gate just before a lane, and head diagonally right to a gap and gate in
the hedgerow. Go straight on to the field corner, through a gate and follow the right side
of a hedge towards some houses. Go down a manicured lane to a minor road. Turn left
and then immediately right to reach a T-junction. Turn right facing a wood and walk
100 yards to a footpath sign for Chorley. Follow the path to the right edge of a wood.
Go through a gate and turn immediately right and follow the field boundary on its left.

After a slight bend go through a gate and diagonally right past some oaks to a double gate. Go straight ahead, aiming for a point about 100 yards left of the farm buildings ahead. At a minor road go left. Beyond the next farm on the right is a footpath sign for Norbury on the right. Scramble through the hedge and go straight across the field to a corner and follow the hedge round towards a corrugated red barn. Just before the barn go through a hedge and make for a gateway in front of a red house. Go right here on a minor road for 100 yards to a footpath sign on the left. Go over a stile and make for a redbrick farm in line with the first short piece of hedge. At Frith Farm go through the farmyard to exit at the rear of the buildings. Go right to a hedgerow and follow this down to the River Weaver (see Walk 43). Cross the river by a cart bridge and go up the opposite bank to a hedgerow. Follow the hedge rightwards for $1^1/_4$ miles, going through the top left of a wood by a tangled lane, and on to another lane. It is now just a short walk past the **Canal Shop** to the start point.

POINTS OF INTEREST:

Marbury Brook – Runs into the Weaver at Wrenbury. Keep an eye out for kingfishers along this stretch.

Garden of Models, Norbury – Quote '*A garden of models including castles, temples, hotels, aircraft, steam engines, ships, trains, cars, towers, monuments, bridges, houses, shops, Disneyland, zoo, animals, birds, guns, ponds, dinosaurs etc.*' Everyone welcome free.

Canal Shop – Craft and gift shop run by English County Cruisers who have a small marina at this site. Open all the main holiday season April-mid November.

REFRESHMENTS:

The Cotton Arms, Wrenbury (tel no: 0270 780377. Food, lunch and evenings. Garden, family room, children and dogs welcome.

The Dusty Miller, Wrenbury (tel no: 0270 780537). Food, lunch and evenings. Restaurant. Children welcome. Dogs confined to outside area.

Walk 71   HIGHER AND LOWER WYCH   6½m (10km)

Maps: OS Sheets Landranger 117; Pathfinder SJ 44/54.

A walk through typical Cheshire farming country. Map and compass highly recommended!

Start: At 496435, the Methodist Church in Higher Wych.

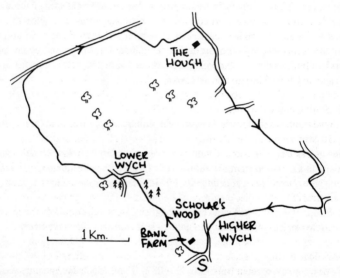

With the church, right and a stream, left, follow the waymark. Go over a stile into a field and bear right uphill towards a farm. Go through a gate at the top, left through a second gate and left of some buildings. Go through two further gates into a field. Go through a gate ahead and, when the hedge on the right turns right, continue to a stile. Go over and left on to a track. Go through a facing gate and bear half-right to a stile at the bottom of the hill. Go over and cross **Wych Brook.** Bear slightly left, entering the next field over a stile. Walk between Scholar's Wood and the brook until a path joins on to the right of the brook. Follow this path to a road by a white house. Turn left to Lower Wych.

At a T-junction go right and, 50 yards past a bridge over a brook and on a right-hand bend, cross a waymarked stile and skirt a rise. Continue with a copse on the right, to join a stream which flows off to the left in a U-bend, returning where the route goes off to the right, the stream still being on the left. Continue on an overgrown path. Go over a bridge, through a gate and then left, up between hedgerows to leave the woods. Follow a faint track with a wood on the left, until a right-hand hedge comes in and the way narrows. Follow the hedge when it bends right and continue to the end of a field. Go through a gate below and to the left. Turn right and continue as before to a gap in the hedge to the right of some pools. There is no stile but it is possible to get over the wire. Go through a gap in the opposite hedge. Turn right and keep with the right edge of the field to a Public Footpath sign. Cross a stile and go right at the road. Go past Wychough House and, on a bend, find a gate to the left of a neglected stile. Go through the gate and keep to the right of the field over a stile into the next field. Go round a pond and on to a corner where you go through the fence. Walk to the right of a hedge and turn left on to a farm track. Pass through a facing gate, bear right, passing a farmhouse on your right, to go through a gate on to the road. Go right for $\frac{1}{2}$ mile to reach a waymarked stile on the left where the road bends right near some houses. Go over and cross two fields, aiming for a farm, then turn left at a road. After 100 yards there is a waymarked stile to the right. Go over, over another stile ahead and cross two fields separated by a gate. Go over a stile on the left and follow a hedge on the right over a farm track to a stile by an oak tree. Go over and aim for a stile ahead. Go over and through a gate left of a pond to a road. Go right. After 300 yards turn right at a bridleway sign and on to a facing gate on a sharp right bend 200 yards further on. Go through and turn sharp left to reach a drive left of a black and white building. Go right to a gate and a stile. Go over and follow the path to where it opens up. There bear right and climb a fence on to a path between two hedges. At an empty pool keep right with a hedge on the left, cross a stile near a gate and join a track which opens out into a field. Turn right, keeping a wire fence on the right and following a fence then a hedge round to the left, ignoring a small gate. Climb down an overgrown bank in front of a copse to reach a bridge and gate. Cross the wire fence at the top of the bank ahead and follow a line of three trees. At the third tree bearing left to a hedge corner. With the hedge close right, continue down a track to a road. Turn left and go downhill to Higher Wych and the car.

POINTS OF INTEREST:
Wych Brook – Once called the River Elfe, it formed the boundary between Cheshire and a corner of what used to be Flintshire. Oldcastle Hill, south of the brook, is the site of one of the border castles that guarded the pass into Cheshire.

REFRESHMENTS:
The Red Lion, Malpas (tel no: 0948 860368).

Walk 72   TARPORLEY AND WHARTON'S LOCK   6¹/₂m (10km)

Maps: OS Sheets Landranger 117; Pathfinder SJ 46/56.

A walk on old bridleways through typical Cheshire country and beside the Shropshire Union Canal.

Start: At 554624, the car park behind the British Legion Club, Tarporley.

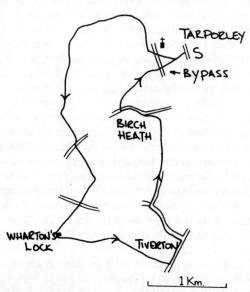

Leave the car park and turn right up the High Street. Just after the Police Station turn left to reach the lych gate of St Helen's Church. Go through a gate and follow the edge of the churchyard to the kissing gate. Follow the path beyond, bearing right beneath the telegraph poles. Go over a stile and walk past the garden of a house. Cross a stile by the gate and walk past a pond and a house. The track bears right along the by-pass. Reach this busy road over the first stile. On the other side, a sign reads 'To Sandstone Trail, Iddenshall'. The way may be obscured by undergrowth, but look for a stile on the left, 10 yards from the roadside. Cross this, turn right and walk between two hedges. After 150 yards you will reach a house on the right. Bear left down the track. About 150 yards from the house turn right through a gap in the hedge and walk to a gap between two hedges 40 yards away. This pleasant bridleway drops gently downhill. You will reach a rather lonely signpost for the Sandstone Trail. Continue in the direction of Beeston Castle and Bulkeley Hill. Cross a double stile and follow a fence on the left. Beeston Castle (see Walk 63) will be seen ahead. Walk in the general direction of the castle, crossing several stiles. The seventh stile leads to a junction of lanes. Go down the facing lane. Cross a stile just before a house on your right and follow the path along a fence, going over a footbridge and across the next field to a lane. Cross the lane and continue with the hedge on your right till you reach the Shropshire Union Canal (see Walk 66) at Wharton's Lock. Cross the canal via the small footbridge above the lower lock chamber, turn left and follow the towpath. (If you were to turn right here you would quickly reach The Shady Oak). After about 1 mile you will reach the road bridge for the A49. Climb to the road here, turn left and walk into Tiverton.

You will reach a cluster of houses on the right called 'The Dale'. Turn right down the footpath signposted 'Tarporley', walking between two earth banks and beneath a canopy of hawthorns. The bridleway ends at a stile into a large field. Go over and cross the field towards a telegraph pole by a tree in the distant corner. Climb a stile and follow the hedge on your left. Cross the next stile and follow a track to Birch Heath. Turn between two houses to reach a lane. Turn left and walk past the farm. Halfway down the hill, a sign by a stile on your right indicates 'Tarporley'. Cross the stile and follow the hedge on the right. Go across the next, narrow field to a facing stile. Cross this, then walk with the hedge on your right for 100 yards. Cross a field towards the church to a stile by a gate in the hedge on your left. Go over and walk along the hedge to the by-pass. Cross the road and the facing stile and follow the hedge on your left to the first hawthorn tree. Cross the stile here and walk to the church, then retrace your steps back to the start.

REFRESHMENTS:

The Swan, Tarporley (tel no: 08293 3838). Situated on the High Street just past St Helen's Church.

The Lock Gate Café (tel no: 08293 2708). Situated by the bridge which carries the A49 over the Shropshire Union Canal. It is open from 9.00am–4.00pm on weekdays, and from 9.00am–5.00am at weekends.

The Shady Oak (tel no: 08293 3159). A good range of food in pleasant surroundings. There is a children's play area.

Walk 73   ALDFORD AND THE RIVER DEE $6^3/_4$m (11km)

Maps: OS Sheets Landranger 117; Pathfinder SJ 45/55.

A pleasant walk along small lanes, old green lanes and the River Dee.

Start: At 419594, near the church at Aldford.

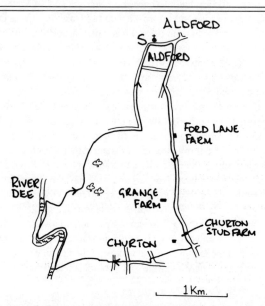

Leave the church and walk into Church Lane. The Post Office is on the right. Go past the telephone box and on to a junction with the B5130. You will see the gates to **Eaton Hall** here, on your left.

Turn right and walk past the Grosvenor Arms. There is an interesting old set of stocks on the other side of the road here. Walk out of the village and turn into the first lane on the left, which has a 'No Through Road' sign at the entrance. Follow the lane to its end where it turns into Ford Lane Farm, just past The Cottage and Brooklands Cottage. Continue straight on, through the facing gateway, and walk the length of the green lane. There is a gate across the straight track near Grange Farm. You are quite likely to see grouse on this section of the walk. The green lane emerges on to a metalled lane at a sharp bend. Turn immediately right here, and cross a stile by a gate. Go across

152

a narrow field and cross a stile and footbridge. Continue between a wooden fence and a hedge, then go down the drive for Churton Stud Farm. Turn left at a crossing lane, and then right opposite Churton Hall. At a crossroads you will see The White Horse, opposite and a little to your right.

Go down Hobb Lane by the pub. This lane becomes a green lane which is followed down to poplar trees by the river bank. Turn right here, cross a stile by the last poplar and go past the small river house. Cross two further stiles and continue along the river bank for $1^3/_4$ miles, as close to the river as the field boundaries allow. A relatively steep arc to the right in the path brings you to a field gateway. Go through and over a footbridge. Walk straight ahead to a gap in the facing hedge. The track, with a hedge on the right, gradually climbs away from the river, then turns right and continues between two hedges. Turn left at the wide entrance into Aldford Hall farm into a small lane. Follow lane for $3/_4$ mile, back to **Aldford Church** and your car.

POINTS OF INTEREST:

Eaton Hall – The residence of the Duke of Westminster, one of the richest men in England. The grounds are sometimes opened to the public.

Aldford Church – The Parish Church of St John the Baptist. A church has stood on this site for centuries. The current one was built in 1884 even though a copper sundial by the door is marked 1708. Behind the church is a mound where a wooden castle once stood, guarding the ford across the River Dee.

REFRESHMENTS:

The Grosvenor Arms, Aldford (tel no: 024465 247). This pub provides bar snacks and Sunday lunches. There is also a restaurant which offers an à la carte menu at a fixed price.

The White Horse, Churton (tel no: 0829 270208). A pleasant pub offering a range of bar snacks.

Walk 74 **Primrose Hill and Willington Corner** 6³/₄m
(11km)

Maps: OS Sheets Landranger 117; Pathfinder SJ 46/56.

A walk on the Sandstone Trail, returning through quiet fields and woods.

Start: At 532680, outside the forest road gate on Waste Lane.

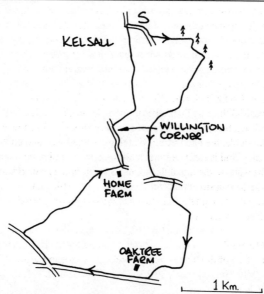

Walk downhill along the forest road to a Sandstone Trail sign indicating a track on the right. Turn here then after 100 yards bear left and uphill. Climb steps to a stile on the right and follow the edge of the field ahead. Go through a kissing gate and cross the next field. Cross a stile and walk along a narrow path between two hedges. Go over another stile and through a gate on to a lane. Bear left for 40 yards to a footpath sign indicating 'Fishers Green, Tarporley'. Take this path (Sandy Lane). The path becomes a gravel track which descends to a lane. Turn left and walk along the lane for 250 yards to a sign on the right for Beeston Castle. Cross a stile and follow the edge of the field ahead. Go over a second stile and follow the hedge on your left.

Cross a stile at the far corner of the field and turn right down the lane. Cross a

154

second stile and follow the hedge on your left to reach a ditch. Bear right and follow the ditch for 200 yards to a Sandstone Trail marker that shows the way over a footbridge and two stiles. Bear right beyond, and follow the ditch to the corner. There bear left and walk along the hedge to a lane. Turn right along the lane, away from the Sandstone Trail, past the turkey houses of **Oak Tree Farm**.

Go ahead at the first crossroads and turn right at the second to pass 'The Beeches', and reach a T-junction. Turn right past 'Holly Bank' and walk on where the lane bears sharp left. Continue ahead on a track. Go through a gate and walk along the cow lane between two hedges. Cross a small stream and go through a gate on the right. Follow the hedge on your left to the corner of a field. Bear right and continue along the edge to the next corner. About 30 yards to the right of this spot is a polished wooden fence beneath a large ash tree. Cross here and walk over the facing field with the hedge on your left until you are able to walk along a concrete track which leads towards Home Farm. The track goes to the dairy so it is best to take care at this point as conditions can be messy underfoot! Go through two gates then turn left and walk to a lane. Turn left. At a crossroads near Willington Post Office turn right up Chapel Lane. Walk uphill, then fork left into Gooseberry Lane. This lane becomes a track leading towards a timber stable. Walk to the stable, then go through a cunning sliding gate and continue up the path ahead. You may find it easier to follow the path by climbing on to and walking along the top of the wall. At the top of the hill cross a stile and go straight ahead across a field. Cross a stile on to a stone track and follow this to a stile on the left. Cross this and walk along the path through the trees to reach Waste Lane by a post box. Turn right and walk up the lane to your car.

POINTS OF INTEREST:
Oak Tree Farm – One of the biggest turkey breeding farms in Europe.

REFRESHMENTS:
The Morris Dancer, Kelsall (tel no: 0829 51291).
Th' ouse at Top, Waste Lane (tel no: 0829 51784).

Walk 75 CHESTER CANAL AND WELSH CANAL 8¹/₂m (13.5km)
Maps: OS Sheets Landranger 118; Pathfinder SJ 65/75.
An easy walk with varied views following the canal towpath, country lanes and footpaths.
Start: At 616566, the Barbridge Inn.

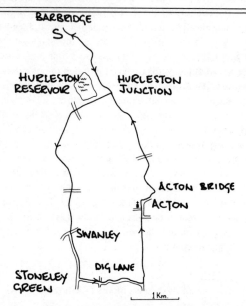

Bridge 100 is adjacent to the inn and offers access to the towpath of the Chester Shropshire Union Canal. Turn right off the bridge and follow the towpath past Hurleston reservoir on the right to Bridge 97. Use the bridge to cross the canal and take the towpath up the **Hurleston Flight** of locks on to the Welsh (Llangollen) Canal. Pause a moment to look back across the Cheshire Plain and forwards to the Pennines.

At Burland (Bridge 6) there is a general store just across the bridge. Continue along the towpath to Swanley. Leave the canal at Bridge 8 and turn right towards Ravensmoor. After passing a wood on the left take the left-hand turn through Stoneley Green. Go straight on at the crossroads and pass Diglane Farm. About 500 yards further, where the lane turns sharply to the right, turn left following the public footpath towards Acton. From this path the Peckforton Hills and Beeston Castle can be seen to

156

the west, with Jodrell Bank Radio Telescope to the north-east and the ground of Dorfold Hall (see Walk 62) immediately to the right of the path. Enter the village of Acton and pass The Star Inn on your left, noting the mounting block outside the inn. Cross the main A534, with Acton Church (see Walk 62) on the left, and take the first turn right. At the bottom of Wilbraham Road, between numbers 27 and 33, take the footpath over a stile and across a field to Bridge 93 of the Shropshire Union Canal. Nantwich basin and its canal shop are only a short walk the towpath if you turn right at Bridge 93, otherwise turn left along the towpath to follow the canal past Hurleston and back to Barbridge.

POINTS OF INTEREST:

Hurleston Flight – A flight of four locks at the beginning of the Welsh (Llangollen) Canal. Unusually, water flows down the canal from the River Dee to be abstracted at Hurleston.

REFRESHMENTS:

The Barbridge Inn, Barbridge (tel no: 027 073 266).

Walk 76   **DANEBRIDGE**   2m (3km)

Maps: OS Sheets Landranger 118; Pathfinder SJ 86/96.

A pleasant walk with fine views that takes you along a river and down winding lanes.

Start: At 965652, on the Cheshire side of the bridge in Danebridge.

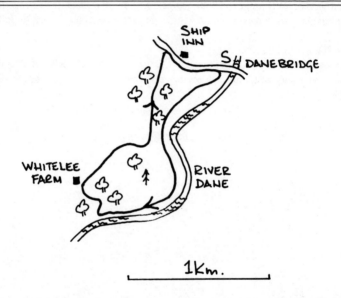

Walk away from the bridge and climb up, passing cottages on the left, to reach steps. Descend these and go down a narrow gully. Go over on to a stile into a field. Continue ahead to another stile. Go over on to a track which bears right. Follow the track which goes close to the **River Dane** for approximately $^3/_4$ mile to arrive at a weir and facing trees. Leave the river at this point and climb to a stone gateway up a slope on the right.

Immediately after passing through the gateway turn left and climb a bank. Go over a stile into a field. Continue climbing, with trees on your right. Leave the field over a stile and follow the signed footpath route through Whitelee Farm. Continue along a track that takes you through five gateways then descends and turns between trees for $^3/_4$ mile. Go right at a crossing road and descend past the Ship Inn and cottages on the right and back to your car.

POINTS OF INTEREST:
River Dane – On the boundary between Cheshire and Staffordshire the river gently wends its way through Congleton and Holmes Chapel entering the River Weaver at Northwich.

REFRESHMENTS:
The Ship Inn, Danebridge (tel no: 0260 227217).

Walk 77   **HOUGH AND WYBUNBURY**   3m (5km)

Maps: OS Sheets Landranger 118; Pathfinder SJ 65/75 & 64/74.

Varied, with conservation, historical, and architectural interest, and the best views of Wybunbury Tower.

Start: At 715506, on a gravelled area near the 30 mph sign in Cobbs Lane by Hough Common.

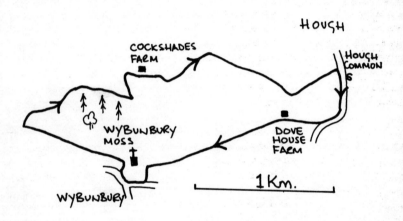

Walk south along the road for 500 yards until you are just beyond Hough House. There a footpath sign on the right leads you into a field. Go diagonally left towards the left corner of Dove Houses Farm. Go over two adjacent fences and a succession of stiles in line with **Wybunbury Church Tower**. As you approach the tower a fenced-off area on the left contains a **moated earthwork**.

Continue towards the tower until you meet a lane. It is now possible to enter the churchyard by a gate up the slope. Alternatively, follow the lane left to the old vicarage then go right up the bank to the Red Lion and right again to bring you to the Swan Inn and the front of the churchyard. Leave the churchyard on its northern side, going through a gate into a field. Turn immediately left and follow the back of the Swan Inn and houses to a stile. Go over and round the back of more houses and past three garages to another stile. **Wybunbury Moss** is the low-lying, tree-filled area below and to your right. Continue along the hedge line until you reach a house apparently blocking the way. Cross the house drive in a direct line with the field fence on your left to arrive at a tree-lined path into the fields beyond. Go along the field edge to reach a lane. Turn right here and descend to the level of the Moss. Follow a lane past a farm and dairy to where it bends left. Go straight on, then over a stile into a field. Follow the left edge to a hedgerow and turn left there over a stile and across a field towards Cockshades Farm.

At the farm turn right and follow a hedgerow to a stile. Go over and along a line of trees towards a fishpond. Skirt the fishpond on its right to the farthest corner and from there take a direct line, following a line of power cables, diagonally left to a wood. Turn right and follow the hedgerow up to the left of Dove House Farm. When the hedge turns left follow it round and take a direct line towards the red brick farmhouse, crossing a small stream on the way. Take the lane on the left of the farmhouse to a road. Turn left along the road to the start point.

POINTS OF INTEREST:

Wybunbury Church Tower – The 15th-century tower has been straightened several times, most recently in February 1989. There has been a church on the site since Domesday.

Moated earthwork – Probably the site of a fortified house used by the Bishop of Lichfield in the 15th century.

Wybunbury Moss – A dangerous area. Do not enter. This conservation site for floating vegetation and trees, birds, butterflies, and bog plants is managed by the Nature Conservancy Council, Shrewsbury.

REFRESHMENTS:

The Red Lion, Wybunbury (tel no: 0270 841277).
The Swan Inn, Wybunbury (tel no: 0270 841280).

Walk 78 RODE MILL AND LITTLE MORETON HALL 3¹/₂m (6km)
Maps: OS Sheets Landranger 118; Pathfinder SJ 85/95.

A short well-marked walk on the urban fringe with fine architectural and historical interest.

Start: At 824575, the church, Rode Mill.

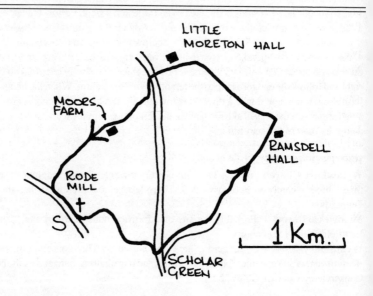

Walk east down the lane at the side of the church and after 150 yards go right through a gate before a stream. Follow a track and turn left before another gate in a fence and go along a hedge to an open field. Continue along the same line across to a stile by two metal gates. Go over and left across a stream. Go up a lane to the main road. Cross and go left up Station Road, following it for 600 yards to a three storey farm. Turn left at a sign for Low Farm and head north toward the Macclesfield Canal. There are good views of **Mow Cop Folly** to the right here.

At a bend by a wood turn up right to meet the canal. Turn left along the towpath for 600 yards to a bridge. Ramsdell Hall is the fine and rambling hall on the opposite bank here. Go left at the bridge by a footpath signed for Moreton Hall and continue, in a more or less straight line, over stiles, which are occasionally rickety. The eerie Great

Moreton Hall appears out of woodland to your right. When you cross a stile by a gate turn left to the magnificent **Little Moreton Hall** and follow signposts for the South Cheshire Way.

At a main road go left for 100 yards then right at a footpath sign in the hedge. Continue over stiles and following the marked footpath signs. Make for a spot about 100 yards to the rear of Boarded Barn Farm. There, follow the field boundary straight on, then left and right to arrive at Moors Farm. Take a lane westwards to the road and Rode Mill. Go left to the starting point.

POINTS OF INTEREST:

Mow Cop Folly – At 1,091ft above sea-level Mow Cop offers extensive views across the Cheshire Plain and beyond. It was built in ruinous style by Randle Wilbraham in 1750 and is associated with the early days of the revival of non-conformism and the establishment of Primitive Methodism.

Little Moreton Hall – Begun in the 15th century, it is one of Britain's finest examples of a timber-framed, moated manor house. There are superb carved gables and recently discovered and restored 16th-century wall paintings.

REFRESHMENTS:

Little Moreton Hall (tel no: 0260 272018). Teas available in season, courtesy of the National Trust. April–September. Children welcome. Dogs to remain outside.

Walks 79 and 80   **AROUND CHURCH MINSHULL** $3^1/_2$m (6km)
or $4^1/_2$m (7km)
Map : OS Sheets Landranger 118; Pathfinder SJ 66/76.
An easy and charming walk with plenty of architectural interest.
Start: At 665605, near the Badger Inn, Church Minshull.

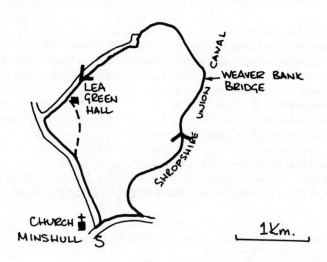

Walk a short way north towards the **church** and turn right on the road to Crewe. Go over
the River Weaver and continue for 600 yards to reach the Shropshire Union Canal. Turn
left along the towpath for approximately $1^1/_3$ miles to reach Weaver Bank Bridge, the
fourth bridge along. Wimboldsley Hall and the Verdin Arms are on your right along
a public footpath, and the main London-Glasgow railway is directly ahead.

At Weaver Bank Bridge go up through a gate and turn right, away from
Wimboldsley Hall, towards woodland. Follow the right-hand edge of the wood, cutting
across at an obvious point. Continue round over stiles and follow a long finger of
woodland to go down to meet the River Weaver again. There are dramatic views of the
river. After 100 yards go left over a wide footbridge across the river and head directly
up to meet a delightful green lane. Continue along the lane until it becomes metalled,

continuing for another $^1/_2$ mile or so to reach Lea Green Hall Farm. A footpath goes through the farmyard and exits at the rear of the yard. Go right down to a wood. Go through the woodland and down to the river. Go right and follow the bank until the wood ends. Continue along a field boundary on your right to reach a road. Go left along the road back to the start point.

An alternative route from Lea Green Hall is to continue along the lane to meet the road. Again go left to reach the start point. This alternative is about 1 mile longer.

POINTS OF INTEREST:

The Parish Church of St Bartholomew, Church Minshull – Commissioned in 1702 and paid for by an extraordinary rate levied on the parishioners. The church contains the vault of the Wades of Wades Green who may have connections with Field Marshal Wade of Jacobite fame.

REFRESHMENTS:

The Badger Inn, Church Minshull (tel no: 0270 71607). An 18th-century coaching inn of historic and architectural interest. Food, lunch and evening. Children welcome. Ask before taking dogs in.

The Verdin Arms, Wimboldsley (tel no: 0270 71275). Food, lunch and evening. Dining area and children welcome. No dogs.

Walk 81　　　　　　ASTBURY　　　　　　3½m (6km)

Maps: OS Sheets Landranger 118; Pathfinder SJ 86/96.

A quiet walk with plenty of variety.

Start: At 846616, the village green in Astbury.

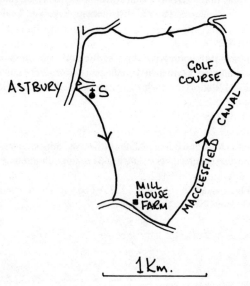

Go down past the green to the main road and turn left. Just past the garage take the footpath up a dirt track. After about 50 yards go into the field on the right, turn sharp left and follow the hedge. At the end of the hedge scan the horizon at about two o'clock to find the ruined folly of Mow Cop (see Walk 78). This will be a useful guide as the walk progresses. Turn right at the end of the field and go through a gap into the next field. Follow the line of the hedge to reach a cattle trough. Go through the gate and straight ahead to another gate in the facing hedge. Go into the next field, face Mow Cop and cross to a stile in the far corner of the field. Go ahead and into the next field. Go over a grass bank and cross a stream by an old footbridge on to a road at a gate. Turn left and go down past Mill House Farm. At an aqueduct go up the rough track by the right support. Go through a hedge and turn left along the canal towpath. Over to the left is the spire of **Astbury Church** and the dish of Jodrell Bank radio telescope.

Follow the towpath under two bridges to a golf course. At a new footbridge connecting the two halves of the course take the path through the wood to reach the course itself at a sign advising walkers to be cautious! Go continuously ahead and follow a line of trees to a footbridge over a small brook. Go up the incline and follow a line of trees across the fairway. Straight ahead is a footpath below a tee. Take this to reach a bridleway where you turn left. Follow the bridleway to a footbridge beyond which the path lies in a hollow to the right, between two rows of trees. This is a recently discovered Roman road, traces of which can still be seen. On emerging from the trees take the narrow path between the fence and the hedgerow to a gate on to a lane. To the right of the farm building go through the tall iron gate by the side of the railings. Follow a footpath to a stile and turn left on to a road. On reaching the main road turn left to return to the lovely village of Astbury.

POINTS OF INTEREST:

Astbury Church – A splendid building dating back to the 14th century and very well preserved. It contains memorials to many famous Cheshire families. During the Civil War Sir William Brereton stabled his horses in the pews, doing considerable damage. In the churchyard is a yew tree said to be a thousand years old. Some of the gravestones have strange symbols on them.

REFRESHMENTS:

The Tea Shop, Astbury, on the A34 at the end of the walk serves light snacks and also sells antiques.

Walk 82   **ALSAGER AND THE MERELAKE WAY**   3³/₄m (6km)

Maps: OS Sheets Landranger 118; Pathfinder SJ 65/75 & 85/95.

An easy to follow mixed walk with a wide variety of flowers and wildlife.

Start:At 807550, the car park at the start of the Merelake Way.

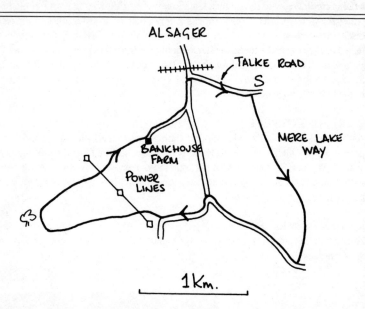

Walk the full length of the line, now the **Merelake Way**, but take the opportunity to climb some of the steps at the side to enjoy the views. At the end of the line turn right on to Merelake Road then left at the T-junction with the main road. Go to the left-hand bend with chevron markings and take the footpath signposted to the right. Follow the brook to a footbridge which is dilapidated but safe to cross. Go ahead with the hedge on your right and pass a pylon to reach a stile next to the third telegraph pole. Go over and continue in the same direction with the hedge on your left. Cross three more stiles. After the third turn right with the hedge on your right to reach a double stile in the corner of the field. Turn left and follow a rough track over two stiles. As a farm comes in view cross a stile on the left and go past the farm, bearing right to reach a track. Follow the track down to Station Road. Turn left, then right into Talke Road to return to the car.

POINTS OF INTEREST:

The Merelake Way – A disused railway line which is one of a number in Cheshire that have been developed for walking and wildlife preservation. It was formerly known as the Audley Branch line and was used mainly for carrying coal from the mines in Stoke-on-Trent although some passenger trains did run. The line closed in 1963 owing to the decline in the mining industry in the area.

REFRESHMENTS:

The Linley Arms, Talke Road, Alsager (tel no: 0270 882732).

Walk 83   THE VALE OF AUDLEM   4m (6.5km)

Maps: OS Sheets Landranger 118; Pathfinder SJ 64/74.

An easy, level walk along towpaths and over fields.

Start: At 659437, the car park near Audlem village centre.

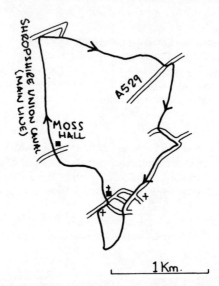

SHROPSHIRE UNION CANAL (MAIN LINE)

A529

MOSS HALL

1 Km.

Leave the car park by the main entrance and turn left away from the village for about 50 yards. Just past the cemetery turn left into a lane opposite the Scout and Guide Headquarters. Continue along this lane for 200 yards and then cross a stile on the left by a waymarked sign. Initially, keep to the left edge of the field, then go straight ahead to a stile when the hedge bends round to the left. On the right is **Moss Hall,** an imposing black and white house.

Cross a further facing stile, then go right and down to the canal, the main line of the Shropshire Union. Go right along the towpath. Continue for about 1$^1/_4$ miles to pass under bridge number 80. Immediately beyond go through an iron gate on the right to reach a farm track. Follow the path to the left down the farm track, keeping straight on through two gates. At a junction of farm tracks go ahead through two more gates and turn right to follow a farm road. After $^3/_4$ mile this joins the A529. Go left for 50 yards, then cross to reach a Public Footpath sign. Go through a kissing gate into a field. Stay on the right of the field and climb a stile to reach a road. Turn right. At a Y-fork go left and, after 200 yards, just past Mill House, turn right. Ignore a facing gate and follow a muddy path past a house on the right. At the end of the path, keep left at a fork and go down to a crossroads. Keep ahead towards the bridge, from where you can see Audlem church, and towards the main road (Stafford Street). Cross and continue down the road ahead for 50 yards, then bear left at a fork. About 10 yards further on you can see The Green and the **Old Grammar School**.

Make for a bridge and a stile at the back of The Green. Go over and turn right. Go over a stile a few yards further on, and go down to a brook. Follow the brook to reach a stile next to a gate. Go over and bear right. Climb the steps to turn right along the towpath which you leave at bridge number 78. Turn right into Shropshire Street and left by **St James' Church** to reach the car again.

POINTS OF INTEREST:

Moss Hall – A timber-framed manor house from the early 17th century. Nuns used to live here and there is said to be a tunnel between the house and the church in Audlem.
The Old Grammar School – A mid 17th-century Elizabethan-style building. It remained a Grammar School until the early part of this century. It is now a private residence.
St James' Church – 13th century and Perpendicular in style. There are marks on the seats of the porch where pikestaffs and swords were sharpened during the Civil War.

REFRESHMENTS:

The Bridge Inn, Shropshire St, Audlem (tel no: 0270 811267). Snacks or main fish and meat dishes daily from 12.00pm–2.00pm. Children welcome. Dogs allowed in main bar only.
The Shroppie Fly, Canalside, Audlem (past the Bridge Inn) (tel no: 0270 811772). A varied menu daily from 12.00pm–2.30pm. Main meals, salads and snacks. Outside seating. Children and dogs welcome. A feature of this pub is the bar made out of a canal longboat.
The Lamb Hotel, Cheshire Street, Audlem (tel no: 0270 811238), also offers food.

Walk 84   **NORTH RODE**   4m (6.5km)

Maps: OS Sheets Landranger 118; Pathfinder SJ 86/97.

A well-defined route offering superb views of the Dane Valley.

Start: At 889665, in North Rode, in the lane between the school and church.

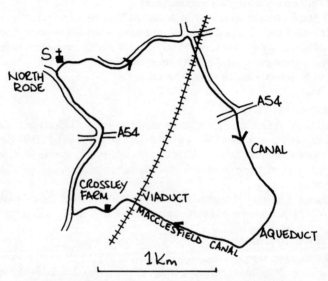

Follow the path straight ahead that takes you round the back of the church. Do not take the path over the cattle grid, but continue round to a stile and go over it into a field. Go straight to another stile. Go over and turn right on to a metalled drive. Follow the drive through a wood and past a lovely lake to a road. Go over a railway bridge and turn right into Station Road. At a T-junction reach the canal towpath through the white gate on your left. Turn right on the towpath and follow it for some distance to the Aqueduct taking the canal over the River Dane where there are spectacular views along the valley.

After crossing the aqueduct leave the towpath at the first bridge and turn right along a farm track. Follow the track down the fields keeping a wire mesh fence on your left. Go through a gate and over a small brook, then through the gate under the spectacular viaduct. Follow the path round to the left to enter the yard of Crossley Farm.

172

Go through the yard, past the barn and leave along the drive. Turn right at the road and go down to the traffic lights. Cross the hump back bridge, then take the footpath into a field on your left. Go over a grassy bank and cross a small footbridge over the river. Turn right and follow the line of the river around the field to reach a stile. Go over and straight ahead to reach a road. Turn left to return to the starting point.

REFRESHMENTS:
The Plough Inn, Eaton (tel no: 0260 280207).

Walk 85 BARTHOMLEY AND ENGLESEA BROOK 4¹/₂m (7.5km)

Maps: OS Sheets Landranger 118; Pathfinder SJ 65/75.
Easy walking, mainly across fields. Paths are not always distinct.
Start: At 768524, the White Lion, Barthomley.

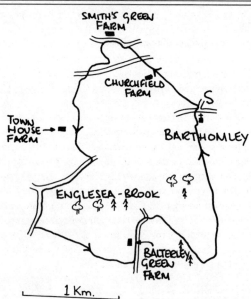

Walk down to the road with the pub on your right and turn right at the T-junction. After 25 yards turn left up a stony drive indicated by a green waymarker sign on the left. Go through a white gate and, where the drive bends to the right, keep forward through a low wooden gate. The path beyond is somewhat overgrown but soon crosses a stile into a field. The route goes straight ahead across a field (there is no track but a Right of Way exists) to a stile to the right of Churchfield Farm. With farm buildings on the left follow another waymarker over a stile and field, keeping to a right-hand hedge. Go over another stile and bear left to a stile in a line of trees. Cross one more stile to reach steps leading to the Barthomley link road. Cross the road to a stile on the other side. Go over and half-left to a stile by a rickety gate. Go over into Mill Lane. Turn left and then right at the T-junction. Pass Smith's Green Farm on the right and in 50 yards climb a green iron ladder on the left by a footpath sign. Go over two further ladders ahead. Continue

174

to a brook and go left, then right and over a brick bridge. Climb the bank on the left and turn right at the top to walk along a hedge and then a barbed-wire fence. Follow the fence around to the left to a stile. Go over and go left of a large pool. Go over the link road again to reach a stile on the opposite side. Go over and bear right, then straight ahead to the left of a spinney. Go over a stile and cross a field. At the field's end turn left and follow the trees around a stagnant pool to reach two stiles and a footbridge. After crossing these, go uphill and over a stile at the top of a bank to the left of Town House Farm. Cross a stile ahead and keep the the right edge of the field to reach a stile. Cross this and turn left to another stile. Go over on to a farm track. Follow the farm track left to a road and turn right towards Englesea Brook. In the hamlet follow the road as it bends sharp left, signposted for Balterley. Pass **Englesea Brook Chapel** on the left and walk uphill for 500 yards.

At waymarker sign on the left pass through a gap in the hedge and cross a field. Go over a footbridge and two stiles separated by a field. Continue through the right-hand iron gate ahead, passing a fish pond to reach Balterley Green Farm track. Turn left into Dean's Lane. After 500 yards, on a sharp left-hand bend, there is a footpath sign on the right. Go over a stile and head towards The Limes farm, keeping to the stream on the right. Go over three more stiles. Now ignore a stile on the right and go over the one on the left. Go over another stile. At this point **Barthomley church** comes into view. Still keeping right, cross a stile in the top right-hand corner of the next field and a further stile ahead on the left. Cross three fields, and three stiles, and in the next field head straight towards the church and a stile. Go over and follow the track past the pond to the church and road. Turn right to rejoin the car.

POINTS OF INTEREST:

Englesea Brook Chapel – Erected in 1828 and extended to its present size in 1832. One of the oldest Primitive Methodist chapels still existing. A schoolroom, added in 1914, contains a small museum of Primitive Methodism. Open Sundays 2.00pm–5.00pm March–October.

St Bertoline's Church, Barthomley – Dedicated to St Bertoline, an 8th-century prince who became a hermit after the loss of his young wife. It was the scene of a massacre in the Civil War when men fled into the church steeple and were almost stifled by the enemy burning the brushes, mats and forms. They were granted quarter but were later brutally murdered.

REFRESHMENTS:

The White Lion Inn, Barthomley (tel no: 0270 882242).

Walk 86   WYBUNBURY AND HATHERTON   5m (8km)

Maps: OS Sheets Landranger 118; Pathfinder SJ 64/74.

A pleasant walk in varied scenery. Watch out for electric cattle fences.

Start: At 700497, the Red Lion, Wybunbury.

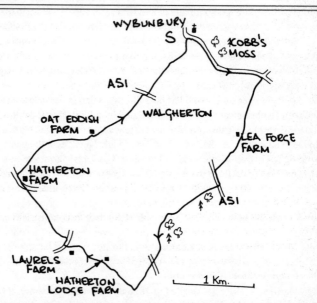

Take the Betley road, passing **Cobbs Moss** on the left. About 100 yards past the entrance to **Wybunbury AC Sand Pit** turn right up a sandy footpath. Go through a gate to reach a pair of gates by Lea Forge farm. Follow the bridleway down to the left, through a gate, on to a metalled road. Pass Lea Forge Trout Farm on your left. At the main road turn right for 100 yards then right again at a sign for Sheepwalks. At the sign for Ballagals go right and follow a lane. Before the next building take the stile on your right and head diagonally left across the narrow field to another stile. Go over, turn left, and go over a stile to reach a footbridge. Take a diagonal line leftwards to the top corner of a wood. Follow this to a stile. Go over and diagonally right to the far corner of the field and a minor road. Cross and follow the South Cheshire Way (SCW) signs until you cross a stile near a new lake. Turn right up to Hatherton Lodge Farm and pass this

176

on its left over a stile. Follow the hedgerow to Laurels Farm. Go through the farmyard by a gate on the right and exit via a car park and two stiles into the farm lane. At a road turn right for 50 yards and take the footpath indicated on your left. Follow the hedgerow, then cross an open field to another field boundary. Continue straight on to cross two more fields to Hatherton Farm.

Turn into the field at the far end of the farm and follow the hedgerow to cross an open field to a gate. Go through this and cross a short field. Go over to a stile in the hedge beyond. Now take a direct line for the right-hand side of Oat Eddish Farm. Turn right up the farm road and after 30 yards go over a stile on the left (Dagfields Farm is 400 yards straight on). Go across the field in the direction of Wybunbury Tower (see Walk 77). Descend to a footbridge and follow the same line to a stile. Go over this and cross the next field leaving a dry pond on your left. Cross a fence and head towards farm buildings, crossing a tiny stream via a footbridge. Follow the left-hand field edge to the farm then cross to a small gate on to the A51. Go right for 100 yards, (the Boars Head is 200 yards straight on) then left by a black and white house. Follow the field edge, always keeping to the left, and where the field dips down go through a gap and across a narrow strip to a stile. Go over this and diagonally right to a metalled lane. Go right to the B5071 and left over the bridge back to the start point. The Swan Inn 200 yards straight on.

POINTS OF INTEREST:

Cobbs Moss – A protected area of reeds, bog, floating vegetation and trees. Rich in plant and bird life.

Wybunbury AC Sand Pit – A good example of how a disused sand pit can be put to some new purpose. Useful bird-watching place from the footpath. No access without permission.

REFRESHMENTS:

The Red Lion, Wybunbury (tel no: 0270 841277). Food, lunch and evening. Children welcome, dogs not.

Dagfields Farm, Walgherton. Home-made farm food. Craft workshops. Children and dogs welcome. Open 10.00am–6.00pm, 7 days, all year.

The Boars Head, Walgherton (tel no: 0270 841254). Food, lunch and evening. Large outside garden and play area. Children and dogs welcome.

The Swan Inn, Wybunbury (tel no: 0270 841280). Food, lunch and evening. Bed and breakfast. Next to the tower. Children and dogs welcome. Outside play area.

Walk 87   **BRERETON GREEN**   5m (8km)

Maps: OS Sheets Landranger 118; Pathfinder SJ 86/96 & 66/76.

A very pleasant walk on level ground with plenty to see.

Start: The car park opposite The Bears Head, Brereton Green.

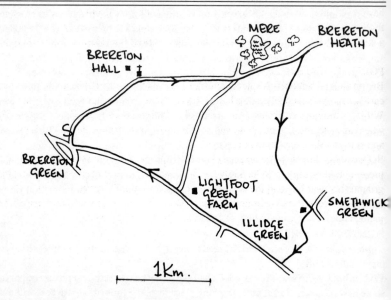

Turn right out of the car park and pass under an archway joining twin lodges and inscribed **Brereton Hall School**. Go straight up the driveway which bears right past the school and the adjoining church of **St Oswalds**. Go past the church and fork right on to a hardcore path. Go through two gates on to a long well made track. Follow the track all the way past a farm, where it turns left, until you reach the end at a T-junction. Cross straight over and enter **Brereton Heath Park** at the signed footpath. Follow the footpath straight ahead, avoiding the many side turnings to arrive at the mere. There is a well-made path around the mere but after enjoying the scene continue on the original path which goes away from the mere through a wood. Cross a stile and turn right on to a bridleway. Keep the fence on your right and follow the bridleway back to the road. Go across the road and over a stile to join a footpath into a field. Keep the wire mesh fence on your left and cross a stile marked 'only use footpath if you know the

178

route'. Go straight ahead and cross a bridge over a small brook. Continue straight across two fields and stiles to where Smethwick Hall Farm comes into view. Cross the last field aiming for the left of the row of trees lining the drive and leave via a gate to emerge on a bend of the road. Turn right and right again into a drive leading to farm outbuildings. Turn left through a gate just before the buildings. Go straight ahead with hawthorns on your left to reach a line of telegraph poles. Follow the poles to a footbridge and stile. Go over and keep the hedgerow on your right. Leave the field over a stile. Turn right on the road which leads back to Brereton Green and the car.

POINTS OF INTEREST:

Brereton Hall School – A splendid building completed around 1600 on the site of an earlier hall. It was modelled on a hall at Rock Savage near Clifton Runcorn where Sir William Brereton, an orphan, was raised. The Brereton family lived here until 1722 when the male line died out. It was taken over as a private school during World War II and enjoys a fine reputation in the area.

St Oswalds Church – The original church dates back to the time of Richard I but the present building only to 1600. Sadly the church is kept locked but a wander round the grounds is rewarding and the key can be obtained from the rectory.

Brereton Heath Park – Formerly a sand quarry, the area is now a country park. The mere is home for a wide variety of birds as well as a sailing club.

Walk 88   **TIMBERSBROOK AND THE CLOUD**   5¹/₄m (8.5km)
Maps: OS Sheets Landranger 118; Pathfinder SJ 86/96.
An easy walk on good paths with some climbing and road walking.
Start: At 895629, the car park at Timbersbrook Picnic Area.

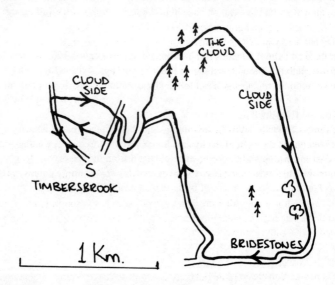

Turn right out of the car park and after about 600 yards go right again down Acorn Lane. At the end of the lane go straight over the crossroads and up Gosberryhole Lane and, as you pass a group of buildings on the right, the track narrows and bears to the left. Keep left when the path forks at a National Trust sign and continue climbing steadily upwards. At the brow of the hill there are good views to the left over the Cheshire Plain towards Jodrell Bank Radio Telescope (see Walk 14) and Alderley Edge. The path enters a wood at a low stone wall and at the junction of four paths. Follow the path on the left marked for Cloud summit, climbing, with the wood on your right for part of the way, to the top. From the trig. point on **The Cloud** the views are magnificent.

Leave the summit (you are now briefly in Staffordshire) and follow the main track in a south-east direction down some steps and over a stile on to a farm track. Turn left and continue down the track to a road. Turn right and along this pleasant minor road through the hamlet of Cloud Side for almost 1 mile, ignoring the road on the left signposted to Woodhouse Green. Shortly afterwards, where the road forks, keep right and continue round to a T-junction. Beware of fast cars as you turn right on to a main road for 250 yards. Turn right again at Bridestones Estate Farm and walk down the farm road to the **burial chamber** on the left.

Retrace your steps to the main road and turn right, then right again 100 yards later when you will see the summit of The Cloud directly in front of you. The road bends sharp left at Springbank Farm. About 100 yards later, it bends sharp left again towards a house, but here you carry straight on for 1 mile, back to the road. Turn left opposite Acorn Lane and after 250 yards turn right and cross a fence/stile leading down a wet, overgrown path to a farm. An iron gate leads into a farmyard and you exit by a farm road leading to the main road. Turn left and retrace your steps to the car.

POINTS OF INTEREST:
The Cloud – To the NNW is Bosley Reservoir and, beyond it, Sutton Common radio mast. The cone to the right of the mast is Shutlingsloe. Rudyard Reservoir lies to the south-east and in a SSW direction beyond Congleton Edge are Mow Cop, Biddulph and the Potteries. On a clear day it is possible to see the Liver Building in Liverpool to the north-west.
Burial chamber – A Neolithic site. The chamber is $18^1/_2$ feet long and is divided into two sections. The semi-circular platform can still be seen. Two smaller chambers were removed in the 18th century.

REFRESHMENTS:
There is nowhere to eat en route but there is an inn on the left of the A54 leading into Congleton.
The Church House, Buxton Road, Buglawton (tel no: 0260 272466). Comprehensive menu of bar meals from 11.30am–2.00pm daily. Children are welcome but dogs not allowed.

Walk 89   TIMBERSBROOK AND RAVENSCLOUGH   5¹/₄m (8.5km)

Maps: OS Sheets Landranger 118; Pathfinder SJ 86/96

A strenuous walk with steep ascents over mixed terrain. Splendid views.

Start: At 896627, the car park in the picnic area, Timbersbrook.

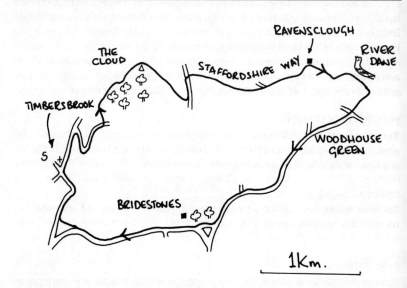

Go through the picnic area then up a flight of steps. Turn left on the road and on reaching the first cottage go into Gosberryhole lane on the right. This leads to the start of a steep hill called Congleton or The Cloud (see Walk 88). At the National Trust sign take the left-hand route. Climb to the top of the Cloud and pause at the trig. point to enjoy the magnificent panoramic views over the Cheshire Plain and Staffordshire Moorlands. Take the path which leads straight on and continue past the National Trust marker down a flight of steps. At the bottom, turn left and descend to a road. Turn left and after about 200 yards a small track leads off to the right to a stile with a small footpath sign. Follow the stone wall through a marshy area to a stile. Go over and continue along a well-worn path past a line of posts. On coming level with some farm buildings descend to the left, go over a stile and turn right. Follow the lane and signs for Ravensclough. On reaching a farmyard go right along a marked footpath. Follow the line of the telegraph wires to find a stile leading into a wooded area with a steep ravine. This is Ravensclough.

The route through the clough is well-defined: at the end of the path cross a footbridge and go straight ahead with the river on your left. The river soon forms a large loop. At the end of the loop on a small ridge take an unmarked footpath to the right. Keep the hedge on your left, then climb the long grass slope to reach a road at the right of the farm house. Take the left-hand fork marked Woodhouse Green. At the end of the lane, by a telephone kiosk, turn left. At the next fork take the road to the left marked Biddulph. After passing a farm take a small road to the right then go right again at a junction. Note the beautiful house and gardens here called The Bridestones. Follow the road to the county boundary then take a footpath to the right marked Tunstall Road. Do not enter the farmyard ahead, but go over a stile on the left into a field. Go straight ahead and follow the stone wall to a road. Turn right to return to **Timbersbrook** and the car.

POINTS OF INTEREST:

Timbersbrook – A mill stood in the heart of the village and was used for silk production and dyeing from 1890 to 1976 when it was demolished. The mill pond is still there and can be seen when returning from the walk.

REFRESHMENTS:

There are no pubs or cafés on the route although there are plenty in Congleton. The route is quite strenuous and it is recommended that you take drinks with you.

Walk 90   WHEELOCK AND MOSTON   5¼m (8.5km)

Maps: OS Sheets Landranger 118; Pathfinder SJ 65/75 and SJ 66/76.

A quiet walk on well-defined routes.

Start: At 750596, at the railway bridge on the A534 above Wheelock.

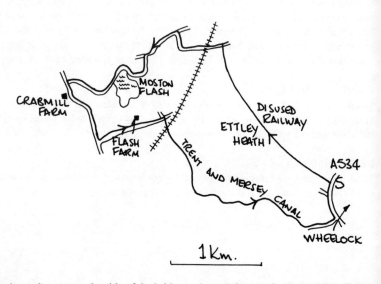

Go down the steps at the side of the bridge and turn left on to the disused line. Follow the line all the way to a mesh fence where a stile leads on to the road. Turn left, then right into Moston Road. At a T-junction turn left and go over the hump-backed bridge. At the next junction turn left over the canal bridge and continue along Plant Lane to a telephone kiosk. Turn left into Watch Lane and follow it round to the right at the 'No Through Road' sign. Pass the end of the mere which forms part of Sandbach **Flashes** and continue along the track to a junction. Turn left and continue to a T-junction. Again turn left, to reach the canal bridge. Turn right on to the canal bank and follow it back to Wheelock Wharf. Turn back on to the main road and up the hill to the starting point.

POINTS OF INTEREST:
Flashes – Moston Flash is one of a series of meres formed by the extraction of salt for which the area is noted. The flashes are very popular with fisherman and are home to a wide variety of birds.

REFRESHMENTS:
The Cheshire Cheese at Wheelock Wharf (tel no: 0270 760319).
The Nags Head, Crewe Road, Wheelock (tel no: 0270 762457).

Walk 91   **WINTERLEY**   5¹/₂m (9km)

Maps: OS Sheets Landranger 118; Pathfinder SJ 65/75.

A very peaceful walk which is easy to follow.

Start: At 747570, the pool in Winterley.

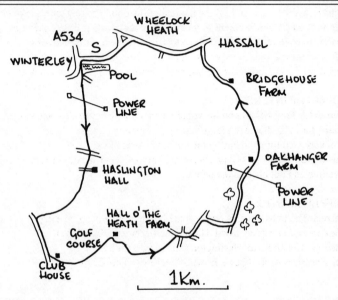

Walk to the Crewe side of **Winterley Pool** and into the lane on the left. At the start of the lane go into a field at a footpath sign. Go up the slope to a stile at the end of the facing hedge. Go over and follow the edge of the market garden into the next field. Go straight ahead to a stile in the right-hand corner. Go over and make for a point between two farm houses where two stiles help you cross a lane to reach a footpath leading straight ahead. Note the beautiful half-timbered **Haslington Hall** amongst the trees to your left.

Cross the farm drive and take the track which is signposted straight ahead. The track ends in a field where there are two footpath signs. Take the path straight ahead and follow it over a series of stiles to enter a farm track leading out on to a lane. Turn left to reach Crewe golf club and take the path to the right, continuing on the grassy track straight ahead. Go to the left of a pond and cross a path to enter a field over a stile in the facing hedge. Go straight on to emerge on to a track which leads to a stile at the side of an iron gate on your left. Go over, turn right in the field and go round to the right of the farm buildings. Pass through the yard avoiding the path to the farm house and leave by the driveway. Turn right on to Holmeshaw Lane and follow to a fork. Go left, and turn right at a house with unusual gateposts mounted with life-like dog's heads. Turn left at a T-junction and enter the driveway of Oakhanger Hall. On reaching a pond turn right across the grass and follow the line of the buildings to a stile. Go over and turn left on a track leading round to a cattle grid. Cross the grid to a metalled driveway leading to Bridgehouse Farm. Go straight through the farm and leave by the drive. Turn left on to the road and at the crossroads turn left again to return to Winterley. Note the beautifully kept gardens of the last house before turning left to return to the car.

POINTS OF INTEREST:

Winterley Pool – Now maintained as a fishery. Day tickets can be obtained from the nearby farm. It is home to a large variety of migratory ducks and geese. At one time the pool was used for baptisms by the church at Wheelock.

Haslington Hall – A well preserved half-timbered house built in 1585. It is a private dwelling and not open to the public.

REFRESHMENTS:

There are no pubs or cafés on the route but the following are nearby:
The Hawke Inn, Crewe Road, Haslington (tel no: 0270 582181).
The Fox, Crewe Road, Haslington (tel no: 0270 582296).
The Foresters Arms, Crewe Road, Winterley (tel no: 0270 762642).

Walk 92   ACKERS CROSSING AND MOW COP   5$\frac{1}{2}$m (9km)
Maps: OS Sheets Landranger 118; Pathfinder SJ 85/95.
A steady climb from the canal to Mow Cop.
Start: At 850589, in the lane near Ackers Crossing.

Go over the crossing and turn right at the end of the lane to reach a canal bridge. Descend to the towpath by the steps at the far side. Turn right under the bridge and continue for about 1$\frac{1}{2}$ miles with the extensive views of the Cheshire Plain on the right, then **Ramsdell Hall** on the far bank and Mow Cop in the distance on the left. Just past the Bird in Hand is a narrow road leading down to the Rising Sun on the right, where you can get light refreshments. A little way beyond the Bird in Hand leave the towpath and cross bridge 86. Go under the railway bridge and follow what looks like an old tram track running down to the canal. At the top of a rise you go into a wood and keep left through it. On leaving, cross two fields (walking close to the right-hand hedge because of boggy land) to reach a road. Turn left to the top of the hill and left again at the T-junction into Mount Pleasant. Beyond some houses the road dips and you will see the village hall on the right. About 300 yards past this is The Brake, a narrow track

188

leading uphill to a rough road.Turn left along the road for a few yards to steps on the right leading up the side of the **Memorial Methodist Chapel** to the village of Mow Cop.

Facing the chapel is a postbox indicating where you should turn left. Turn right immediately by the side of a three-storied building which used to be a velvet mill. The path winds round the back of some houses, bears right then left beneath a solitary house to Mow Cop Folly (see Walk 78). Do not use the small paths as they may be loose underfoot. From this point you can see as far as Wales and Shropshire to the west and south-west and the Derbyshire hills to the north-east. Directly to the north can be seen the Old Man of Mow, a splinter of gritstone.

From the castle head towards the Old Man until you reach Castle Street. Turn left, and just over the hill is a signpost on the right indicating Ackers Crossing. Take this path that leads to the west of the Old Man and in a few yards a further sign points downhill to the left. It is worth stopping here to look at the unhindered view towards Congleton and the Peak District. Jodrell Bank Radio Telescope can also be seen on a clear day. Follow the downward path across a field and through woods to return to the lane from which you started.

POINTS OF INTEREST:

Ramsdell Hall – A mid 18th-century country house with unusual architectural features including an octagonal dining room and hexagonal hall. Privately owned.

Memorial Methodist Chapel – Stands in Primitive Street as a reminder of Mow Cop's part in the emergence of the Primitive Methodists as a separate sect. Camp meetings were held on the hill top.

REFRESHMENTS:

The Rising Sun, Kent Green, Scholar Green (tel no: 0782 776235). Bar snacks Monday-Saturday. Full Sunday lunches. Children welcome. Dogs in bar only.

Walk 93   ASTBURY   6¹/₂m (10km)

Maps: OS Sheets Landranger 118; Pathfinder SJ 86/96 & 85/95.

A most enjoyable walk down a canal towpath and over farmland.
Not strenuous.

Start: At 846615, the village hall car park, Astbury.

Leaving the car park go left passing Glebe Farm, and Rose Cottage. At a fork in the road go right. Continue past Bank Farm to arrive at the Macclesfield Canal by bridge 80. Leave the lane here to take the towpath, going right under the bridge. Go under bridges 82, 83, 84 and 85. After about ¹/₂ mile you will arrive at a bridge that is not numbered. Leave the canal side here, over a stile on the right, to follow a signposted route to Little Moreton Hall. The route is well-defined, following a track to a stile at the side of a field gate. Go over and turn right, walking with a hedge on your immediate right.

Keeping farm buildings ahead cross three stiles and pass close to the farmhouse. Go over a stile which leads to the entrance drive of Little Moreton Hall (see Walk 78). Continue down the drive to meet a crossing road. Turn right, pass Cuttleford Farm on your left, and walk ahead for 100 yards to turn left through a field gate. Continue with a hedge on your left at first, then across a field through a gap in the hedge to meet a facing gate. Go through on to a lane. Turn right, shortly passing Alcumlow Hall Farm drive. Go left here at a fork in the lane to cross a stream and arrive at a junction. Go left, then right at the side of houses down a gravel track which leads on to a track. Continue to a crossing lane. Cross over this and skirt to the left of a green area. Continue, passing dwellings and a farm on your left. Go right, at the side of a large barn, down a winding grassy track. Do not leave this track as you pass footpath signs and field gates, but continue to reach a stile at the side of a facing gate that ends the track. Go over into a field. Skirt this field arriving at a double stile. Go over and cross the next field with a hedge on your right to reach a stile in a facing hedge. Go over and right down a narrow lane to arrive at a crossing road. Go right, then left and back to your car.

POINTS OF INTEREST:

Relics of the Cheshire man have been found in this area. These include tools dating back to the Neolithic age and implements of the Bronze Age found near Congleton.

REFRESHMENTS:

Little Moreton Hall (tel no: 0260 272018). Teas available in season, April–September.

Walk 94   SWETTENHAM   6¹/₂m (10km)

Maps: OS Sheets Landranger 118; Pathfinder SJ 66/76.

A picturesque walk with magnificent views of the Cheshire countryside.

Start: At 774678, 1 mile from the centre of Holmes Chapel near the railway viaduct on the A535, at a sign for Twemlow.

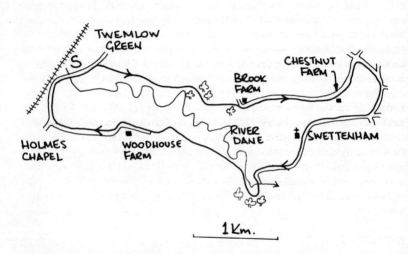

Cross the road and go over a stile where the way is a signposted footpath route to Swettenham. Keep to the left of the field with a hedge on your left. Cross another stile and go straight across the next field to a gate. Go through and descend through trees to cross a stream. Climb up the bank diagonally to a facing gate. Go through and bear right to cross a stile at the top of a slope. Keep forward for 100 yards and cross a further stile. Bear left and climb to skirt around trees on the right to a stile at the side of a gate. Go over and follow a fence on your left. The path bears right and descends through trees. Climb up a facing bank and go through a gate in a crossing hedge. Go through another gate in a crossing fence and bear left along a field track which skirts around a wooded hill to your left. Climb the bank on the left to continue along a higher ground with a fence on your left. Skirt farm buildings, following a footpath sign to reach a lane over a stile. Turn right, passing Brook Farm House on your left, and go through two gates. Go down a grassy track, passing a farmhouse on the left. Go through a gate and continue, passing Chestnut Farm on the right, into a Nature Reserve.

The track now becomes stony and leads into a lane. Go ahead, but shortly before you reach a crossroads turn right through a field. Walk in the direction of a line of four oak trees and cross a stile on to a farm track. Go left, then right following the lane. Continue, following the Swettenham sign, then descend to cross over Midge Brook. Swettenham Mill is on your left here, but the way is straight ahead, climbing slightly to enter a joining lane on your right. Go past Swettenham cemetery on your left and continue down a 'No Through Road'. Soon you pass through a gate at the side of a small house and go over the River Dane via a small bridge. Follow a facing track for 200 yards, then climb a bank on your right to cross a stile into a wood. Follow a well-defined track through the wood emerging into a field. Skirt the field, keeping trees on your immediate right for 150 yards. Now take a path on the right that descends into woods, dropping to a stile. Go over and with trees on your left, go left to cross open ground. Keep ahead, leaving the riverside and making for the facing trees. Cross a small stream and climb a facing bank. Go over a double stile. Go right following a track with the fence on your right. Pass through gates over a track to enter a field. Cross the stile in the diagonally right corner of the field. Descend and cross a small stream, then climb up and go through a facing gate. Go left through a second gate and forward on an uphill track that shortly bears right, passing Woodhouse Farm on your left. Follow the track as it winds to meet the Holmes Chapel–Twemlow Road. Go right now for $1/_2$ mile back to your car.

REFRESHMENTS:
Food and facilities are available at the very friendly pub in the village, called the *Swettenham Arms* (tel no: 0477 71284), where the landlord makes you most welcome.

Walk 95   HANKELOW AND BROOMHALL $7\frac{1}{2}$m (12km)

Maps: OS Sheets Landranger 118; Pathfinder SJ 67/74.

A very pleasant walk.

Start: At 672455, near the village green in Hankelow.

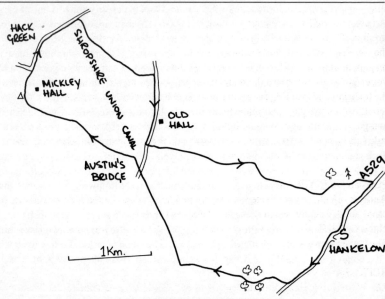

Walk down the main road towards **Audlem** past the White Lion pub. At a footpath sign on a private road to Hankelow Mill turn right and follow the road to the Mill and a bridge over the River Weaver (see Walk 43). Head on up the farm track and where it bends right go straight on over two fields to a visible canal bridge (Bennett's Bridge). Turn right here along the towpath of the Shropshire Union Canal (see Walk 66) going under a road. Where the old railway crossed the canal go up on to the bridge (Austin's Bridge) and over the canal. Follow the South Cheshire Way (SCW) signs over a stile into a field. Cross the field and go over two more stiles. Follow the field boundary on the left to a small shrubby hedge and turn right for 50 yards. Go left over a stile by a small pond. Take the field hedge on your right and go over a stile by a gate. Make directly for a hedge corner some 150 yards ahead and leave the field over another stile at a gate. The South Cheshire Way goes left here, but you go straight on along the hedge past a trig. point, with Mickley Hall on the right. Go through a gate and down a short lane to meet a minor road. Continue along the road for $^2/_3$ mile to cross the canal. A footpath sign on the right points the way through a gate and over several stiles past the WT station and the regional seat of government. **Hack Green Pool** is on your right.

Continue along the forbidding wire fence, then follow a hedgerow to go over a stile. Go directly across to another stile. Go over and diagonally right to a gate. Go through and follow the hedgerow to exit by a gate on to a road. Go right for $^2/_3$ mile to reach the SCW signs at a hedgerow on the left just beyond Westview Cottage. Follow the signs across three fields. Go through a gate and turn right down to another gate. Go diagonally right to a stile in the corner of the field. Go over and keep the boundary on your right to go over two stiles and then a cart bridge over the River Weaver. Follow the track beyond the bridge to a stile. Go over and climb up with the boundary on your left. Go through a gate and follow the boundary on your right to a lane. Cross the lane and go over a stile to woodland. Bear left across a fence and two fields and go over a stile to a house. Continue over another stile and down a driveway to meet the A529. Turn right here back to the start point.

POINTS OF INTEREST:

Audlem – A charming village with a fine church and several good pubs and hotels. A canal holiday centre with a succession of locks.

Hack Green Pool – Worth visiting if only to read the list of things you cannot do here. The owner seems to be a character.

REFRESHMENTS:

The White Lion, Hankelow (tel no: 0270 811288). Food, lunchtime and evenings. Dining room at weekends. Children welcome. No dogs.

Walk 96 **HANGING GATE AND THE GRITSTONE TRAIL** 8m (13km)
Maps: OS Sheets Landranger 118; Pathfinder SJ 86/96.
*A varied walk through gritstone country, passing ancient
settlements and with magnificent views in all directions.*
Start: At 953697, near the Hanging Gate pub.

Go south for 100 yards and turn right over a stile. Go diagonally left down the field to
the left bottom corner. Continue left along the old green lane and follow the field
boundary to where a lane comes in from the right. Carry straight on at this point to a
footbridge over a stream and a 'squeezer' among some trees. Go up the slope ahead to
cross below a farm. At the left of the farm pick up an old track going left on the far side
of a wall. Go through a gate and go ahead, making for the left of the trees ahead to reach
a minor road. Turn left up the hill to a T-junction. About 300 yards along the road to
the right is **Cleulow Cross**, among some trees.

Go straight over at the junction and follow a signed footpath rightwards and then
an old track to Long Gutter Farm. At the main road turn left for 200 yards to the Wild
Boar pub. Follow a footpath sign opposite the pub over a stile and straight down the

hill to the right of the wood. (Beware of clay pigeon shooters here). Go diagonally up left to a stile about 300 yards left of the farm. Go straight across the road and down the lane opposite to a point where the lane makes a sharp left turn. Go straight on at this bend over a cattle grid and follow a lane down to the farm. A finger post just before the farm points the way down towards the stream in Greasley Hollow. Follow the stream on its left and then cross over to follow its right bank for 300 yards until the path climbs away from the stream and another track leads off right up the bank. Take this second track passing to the right of a ruined and deserted farm. Take the lane behind this farm up to the top of Wincle Minn. Once on the ridge there are magnificent views in all directions. Turn right along the Gritstone Trail towards the British Telecom tower. At the main road turn left for 100 yards and then right up a lane towards the tower. Follow the ridge by lanes and over stiles, gradually descending to reach a large walk-over stile on your right. Go over this and down past a farm to a road. Turn right for 150 yards, then left over a stile by a house and follow the Gritstone Trail to another minor road. Go right here for 150 yards up the hill and take a footpath on the uphill side of the house on the right. This leads to the Hanging Gate pub and the start of the walk.

POINTS OF INTEREST:

Cleulow Cross – A Saxon cross still standing on a knoll among trees. It was used as a Roman beacon.

REFRESHMENTS:

The Hanging Gate, Hadden, Sutton (tel no: 02605 2238). Food, lunch and evening. Cosy. Outside eating. Children welcome. No dogs.

The Wild Boar (tel no: 0260 227219). Spacious pub that does food 10.00am–2.00pm and 7.30pm–10.00pm. Children welcome. No dogs. Sundays very busy.

Walk 97   HOLMES CHAPEL AND BRADWALL   8$\frac{1}{2}$m (13.5km)

Maps: OS Sheets Landranger 118; Pathfinder SJ 66/76.

An easy to follow route mainly on quiet country roads.

Start: At 762673, the Holly Lodge Hotel at the traffic lights on the A50.

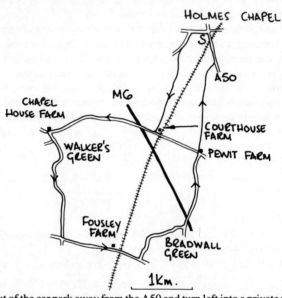

Turn right out of the car park away from the A50 and turn left into a private road called The Drive. At its end climb over a stile into The Southlands. Turn left and after a short distance take the footpath on the right. Go through some stumps on to a metalled drive which leads down into the fields by a post box. Follow the well-marked path through the field and bear round to the left to a footbridge over the river. Go ahead to a gap in the hedge. Go through and across a dry ditch. Continue with trees on your right. At the end of the field turn right and follow the hedgerow to the fence. Go through a gap and turn left through a gate. Go diagonally right across the field, then follow the hedgerow to a fence and cross the narrow field to a gap in the hedge.

Continue ahead to reach a farm and turn right on to the road. Go over the motorway bridge and continue to Jones' Lane on the left. Take this, and at its turn left towards

Bradwall. Go over the railway bridge and turn left into Walnut Tree Lane. At the end turn left over the motorway and continue to the T-junction. Go over towards Pewit Farm straight ahead along a footpath to Alum Bridge. Enter the farmyard and go into the field on the left. Go diagonally left to a stile, then follow the fence to a gap in the hedge. Cross several fields and stiles. When in sight of the road cross a stile on the left and follow the path to the road. Turn left to **St Luke's Church** and the start.

POINTS OF INTEREST:

St Luke's Church, Holmes Chapel – In the town centre and well worth a visit. It was built in the 14th century and the main tower is mainly original. There are bullet marks on the lower part from the Civil War.

REFRESHMENTS:

The Holly Lodge Hotel, London Road, Holmes Chapel (tel no: 0477 37033).
There are a number of other pubs and restaurants in the town.

Walk 98   **WARMINGHAM MOSS** $8^3/_4$m (14km)

Maps: OS Sheets Landranger 118; Pathfinder SJ 66/76 & 65/75.

A long walk across pleasant countryside. No ascents but plenty of stiles.

Start: At 709611, the Bear's Paw, Warmingham.

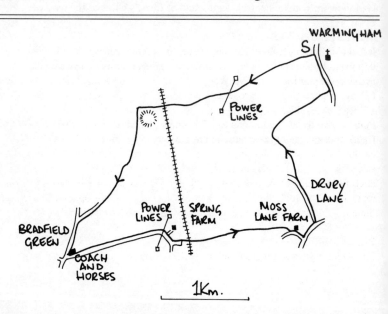

Leave the car park and turn right to reach a phone box. Take the footpath next to it. Follow the river bank to a gate. Go through and straight across the field to a stile. Go over and up the bank and cross two more fields and stiles. On entering the third field follow the row of trees that converges with the power lines and pass under the lines to reach a stile. Go over and ahead to another stile. Go over this, a footbridge and a stile next to an oak tree. Go through a gate and follow the hedgerow round to a narrow strip of land known as a *slang*. At the end of the slang go through a gap and turn left following the hedgerow to a footbridge over the railway.

   A stile at the end of the next field leads on to a farm track. Do not go through the gate here, but cross the bridge over the ditch at the side of it and follow the hedgerow round over a series of stiles. As the old pylons diverge to the left go through a stile in the facing hedge and keeping the hedge on your left go over a footbridge on to a hard track leading to a farm building. Ignore the footpath to the left and go into the farmyard then turn left on to the road. After enjoying a noggin at the Coach and Horses turn left into Moss Lane. There is a long straight stretch after which the lane bends to the right. Here take the driveway of Springfield Cottage. As the drive bends to the right take a footpath over fields to a bridge over the railway. Go straight ahead over a series of stiles and across a driveway and field to reach Moss Lane Farm and the main road. Turn left and then left into Drury Lane. Take the second footpath, where the lane bends to the left, and cross a long field to a stile in the facing hedge. Go over and follow a well-defined track. Go over another stile and turn right past a pond. Go through two fields and over a footbridge. Cross the field to emerge on the main road. Turn left to return to Warmingham and the start point which is close to the village **Craft Workshops**.

POINTS OF INTEREST:

Craft Workshops – These occupy an old mill which has existed since 1289. The current building dates back to 1780 and houses a fascinating gallery of craft items for sale. Visitors can see many of the items being made on the premises. There is also an aircraft museum where old planes and engines can be seen in various stages of renovation. The mill is up the hill from the Bears Paw. It is only open on Saturdays and Sundays. Further details can be obtained by telephoning 0270 77304.

REFRESHMENTS:
The Bears Paw, Warmingham (tel no: 0270 77317).

Walk 99 CHURCH MINSHULL AND WETTENHALL 9m (14.5km)
Maps: OS Sheets Landranger 118; Pathfinder SJ 66/76.
A long walk along pleasant footpaths and quiet roads.
Start: At 666605, the Badger Inn, Church Minshull, a listed building.

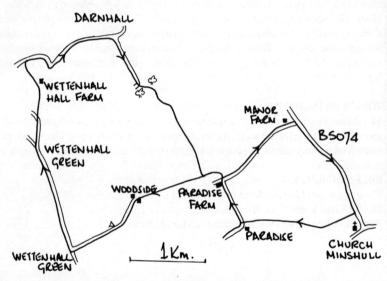

Turn left out of the car park and follow the road round to a bridge. Take the path to the left which leads to the garden of a private house. A Public Footpath leads from the garden's left-hand side to a field. Go straight ahead to a farm track which leads past a small wood to reach a gate. Leave the path through the gate and go up the bank to a water trough. Cross the fence at this point and then go through the gate across the field to your right. Go diagonally to the left and through a gate to the farm and out on to the road at a bend. Turn right and follow the road to the next bend. Turn into the farm drive then go across the field to your right, going over two stiles. Turn left and follow the hedgerow for two fields before crossing to the other side of the hedge and continuing in the same line to reach a farm building where a track and gate lead on to a lane. Follow the lane to a road and turn right through Wettenhall to the Boot and Slipper pub.

Continue along the same road to a left-hand bend with chevron marker and enter the field ahead of you. Cross to a footbridge, go over it and up the bank to a gate. Go through and cross the field to Wettenhall Hall Farm. Enter the field to the left of the farm and follow the perimeter fence past a slurry pit and continue to a disused gate leading on to the road. Turn right and follow the road for some distance to a telephone kiosk outside Darnhall Village Hall. Take the footpath opposite the hall along Smithy Bank Road. Continue on along a driveway and bear left through a wooded area. After climbing a steep path out of the wood take the path to the left which leads to the base of a **Radio Telescope**. A short distance before a gate cross the field to your right to reach a stile with a ditch. Go over and turn left to another stile. Go over and turn right, and following the hedgerow through two fields, then crossing a third to return to Paradise Farm. Turn left on to a lane and follow it to the main road. Turn right to return to Church Minshull about 1 mile away.

POINTS OF INTEREST:

The Radio Telescope – One of a number belonging to the University of Manchester and controlled from Jodrell Bank. It is used to gauge the distances of astronomical radio sources on a triangulation basis in conjunction with others in Sweden and America.

REFRESHMENTS:

The Badger Inn, Church Minshull (tel no: 027 071 607). A listed building.
The Boot and Slipper Inn, Wettenhall (tel no: 027 023 238).
Both are old coaching inns and offer a full range of menus.

Walk 100   **AROUND BRIDGEMERE**   12m (19km)

Maps: OS Sheets Landranger 118; Pathfinder SJ 65/75 & 64/74.

A long walk on footpaths and minor roads.

Start: At 715506, the gravelled area by Hough Common on Cobbs Lane near the 30 mph sign.

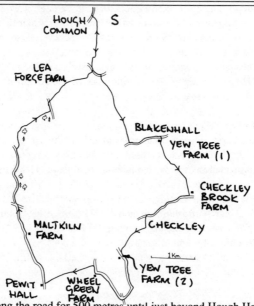

Walk south along the road for 500 metres until just beyond Hough House. Take the footpath on the left before three 'semis', going over two stiles. Keep right of the boundary and where it bends left, head straight across the open field to a farm track 200 yards right of a farm. Follow the left side of a hedge downhill to a stream. Go right over a stile and, in 50 yards, left over another and up the slope to a minor road. Turn left for 200 yards to reach a footpath sign on the right. Follow this, skirting round the back of the newly acquired garden and going left to a stile. Go over and follow the hedge to a gate. Go through and diagonally right of the wood, then straight on to another gate. Go through and follow the hedge on your right to a lane and minor road at Blakenhall. Go left for 500 yards to a left-hand bend near Yew Tree Farm. There, take a footpath on right. After 30 yards go over a stile in 30 yards and follow the hedge to the second right-angled bend. Cross the boundary on to a farm lane and follow this down for 100 yards. Turn left and make for a small gate in the hedge. Go through this and follow the left-hand field boundary through two gates. Head diagonally right to exit down a green lane to Checkley Brook Farm. Go right through the village at Checkley and turn left at Bank Top Farm. Look for a footpath sign on right after 300 yards. Follow this, taking a direct line across a field and descend over a fence to reach a footbridge. Go over the bridge and slightly left up a bank to an awkward stream crossing. Beyond is an overgrown green lane. Avoid this on its left until you can re-enter it easily and follow it to a minor road. Go left along this road to the A51. (**Bridgemere Garden Centre** is 200 yards to the left here.)

Cross the main road and go along the road opposite. After $^2/_3$ mile, just past Wheel Green Farm and a new house, turn left up a lane. Continue in the direct line of this lane to Pewit Hall. Enter the farmyard along the right-hand side of the pond, go through the yard and exit right along the road to Hatherton. After about $1^1/_2$ miles, cross a junction and continue for $^2/_3$ mile to a footpath sign for the South Cheshire Way (SCW) on the right. Follow the Way past a wood and over a footbridge. Go up the far side, over three stiles and down a lane to the A51. Go left for 100 yards then right to Lea Forge Trout Farm. Continue up the bank for 100 yards, then turn right to reach a stile. Go over and turn left to follow the field boundary to Lea Hall Farm. Go left around buildings and through a double gate. Go left through a gate on to a concrete drive that leads to a minor road. Go left and in 50 yards turn right and retrace the first $1^1/_3$ miles of the walk.

POINTS OF INTEREST:

Bridgemere Garden Centre – Reputedly Europe's largest. It has a cafeteria that serves a variety of tasty, attractive, and healthy foods.

REFRESHMENTS:

The Bridgemere Garden Centre (tel no: 09365 381). Open all year. Children welcome. No dogs.